dabblelab

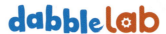

Manga Drawing with

DC

HOW TO DRAW WONDER WOMAN MANGA!

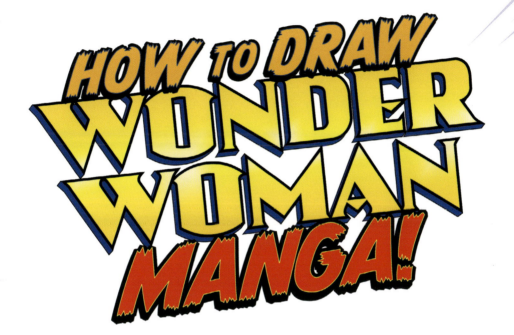

by Christopher Harbo

illustrated by Giulia Campobello
cover artwork by Haining

Wonder Woman created by William Moulton Marston

CAPSTONE PRESS
a capstone imprint

Published by Capstone Press, an imprint of Capstone.
1710 Roe Crest Drive
North Mankato, Minnesota 56003
capstonepub.com

Copyright © 2023 DC.
WONDER WOMAN and all related characters and elements © & ™ DC. (s23)

All rights reserved. No part of this publication may be reproduced in whole or in part, or stored in a retrieval system, or transmitted in any form or by any means, electronic, mechanical, photocopying, recording, or otherwise, without written permission of the publisher.

Library of Congress Cataloging-in-Publication Data
is available on the Library of Congress website.
ISBN: 9781669021735 (hardcover)
ISBN: 9781669021698 (ebook PDF)

Summary: Wonder Woman and manga unite! Put a new spin on mythical Super Heroes and Super-Villains and learn how to draw them as dynamic manga characters with easy-to-follow steps.

Editorial Credits
Editor: Abby Huff; Designer: Hilary Wacholz;
Media Researcher: Jo Miller; Production Specialist: Tori Abraham

Image Credits
Photos: Capstone Studio: Karon Dubke 5 (all), Backgrounds and design elements: Capstone

Inks by Salvatore Di Marco and Giulia Campobello
Colors by Francesca Ingrassia

The publisher and the author shall not be liable for any damages allegedly arising from the information in this book, and they specifically disclaim any liability from the use or application of any of the contents of this book.

Printed in the United States   5666

TABLE OF CONTENTS

MARVELOUS MANGA! 4

THE MANGAKA'S TOOLKIT 5

WONDER WOMAN 6

STEVE TREVOR 8

ETTA CANDY 10

QUEEN HIPPOLYTA 12

PHILIPPUS 14

THE CHEETAH 16

ARES 18

CIRCE 20

GIGANTA 22

DEVASTATION 24

MORGAINE LE FEY 26

WONDER WOMAN VS. GORILLA GRODD . . . 28

MORE MANGA DRAWING FUN! 32

MORE DC SUPER HERO FUN! 32

MARVELOUS MANGA!

Wonder Woman has protected humanity, battled mythical gods, and preserved world peace for more than 80 years! In that time, she has captivated fans through comic books, TV shows, and feature films. But what's one popular print medium Princess Diana has seldom graced? The panels of marvelous manga.

Manga is comics and graphic novels created in Japan. And it's been around longer than Wonder Woman. Much longer, in fact! The very beginnings of the manga art style trace back to a set of painted scrolls from around 1200 CE! But the modern manga we love today really took off in the late 1940s, in magazines and books. Since then, manga has become famous for stylized characters with large eyes, small noses and mouths, and pointed chins. And the types of stories these Japanese comics can tell are limitless. Action and adventure. Comedy and history. Science fiction and romance. Manga has something for everyone!

SO WHY NOT BRING THE MARVELS OF MANGA TOGETHER WITH WONDER WOMAN? NOW YOU CAN! DRAW YOUR FAVORITE MYTHICAL SUPER HEROES AND SUPER-VILLAINS IN MANGA STYLE!

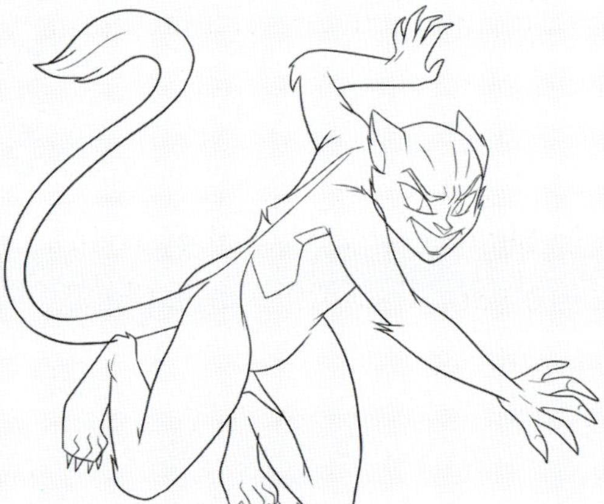

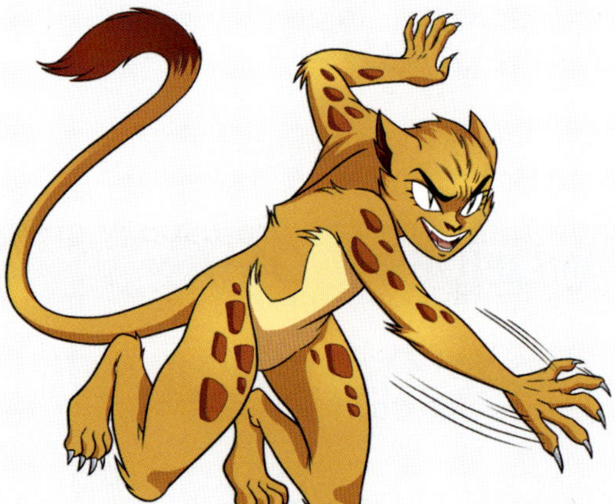

THE MANGAKA'S TOOLKIT

All manga artists—or mangaka—need the right tools to make amazing art. Gather the following supplies before you begin drawing:

PAPER

Art supply and hobby stores have many types of special drawing paper. But any blank, unlined paper will work well too.

PENCILS

Sketch in pencil first. That way, if you make a mistake or need to change a detail, it's easy to erase and redraw.

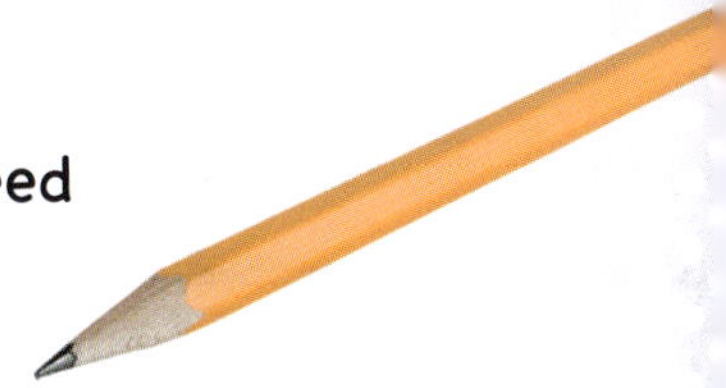

PENCIL SHARPENER

Keep a good pencil sharpener within reach. Sharp pencils will help you draw clean lines.

ERASERS

Making mistakes is a normal part of drawing. Regular pencil erasers work in a pinch. But high-quality rubber or kneaded erasers last longer and won't damage your paper.

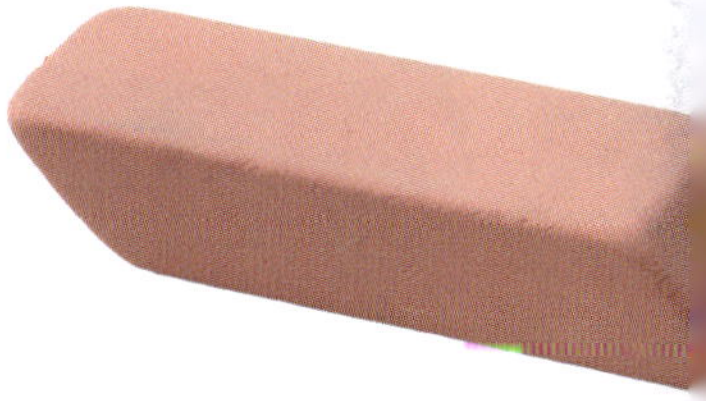

BLACK MARKER PENS

When your sketch is done, trace over the final lines with a black marker pen. By "inking" the lines, your characters will practically leap off the page!

COLORED PENCILS AND MARKERS

While manga stories are usually created in black and white, they often have full-color covers. Feel free to complete your manga masterpiece with colored pencils and markers. There's nothing like a pop of color to bring characters to life!

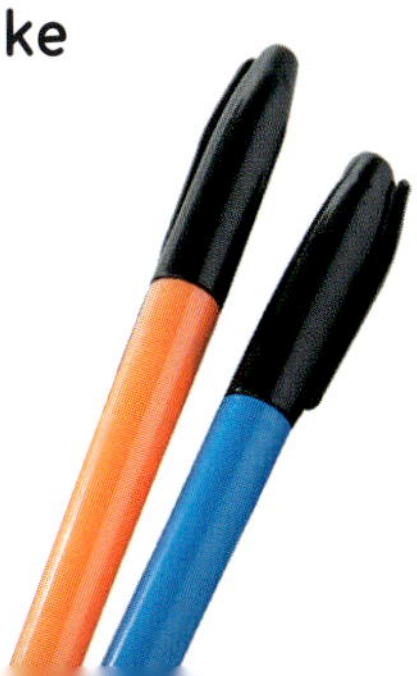

WONDER WOMAN

When the world gets walloped by the wicked, Wonder Woman is a warrior who never wavers. Blessed by the Greek gods, Princess Diana boasts super-strength, lightning reflexes, and the power of flight. But her greatest tool for foiling felons may be her magnificent magic lasso. With its golden coils, the Amazing Amazon can compel even the most tight-lipped troublemaker to tell the truth!

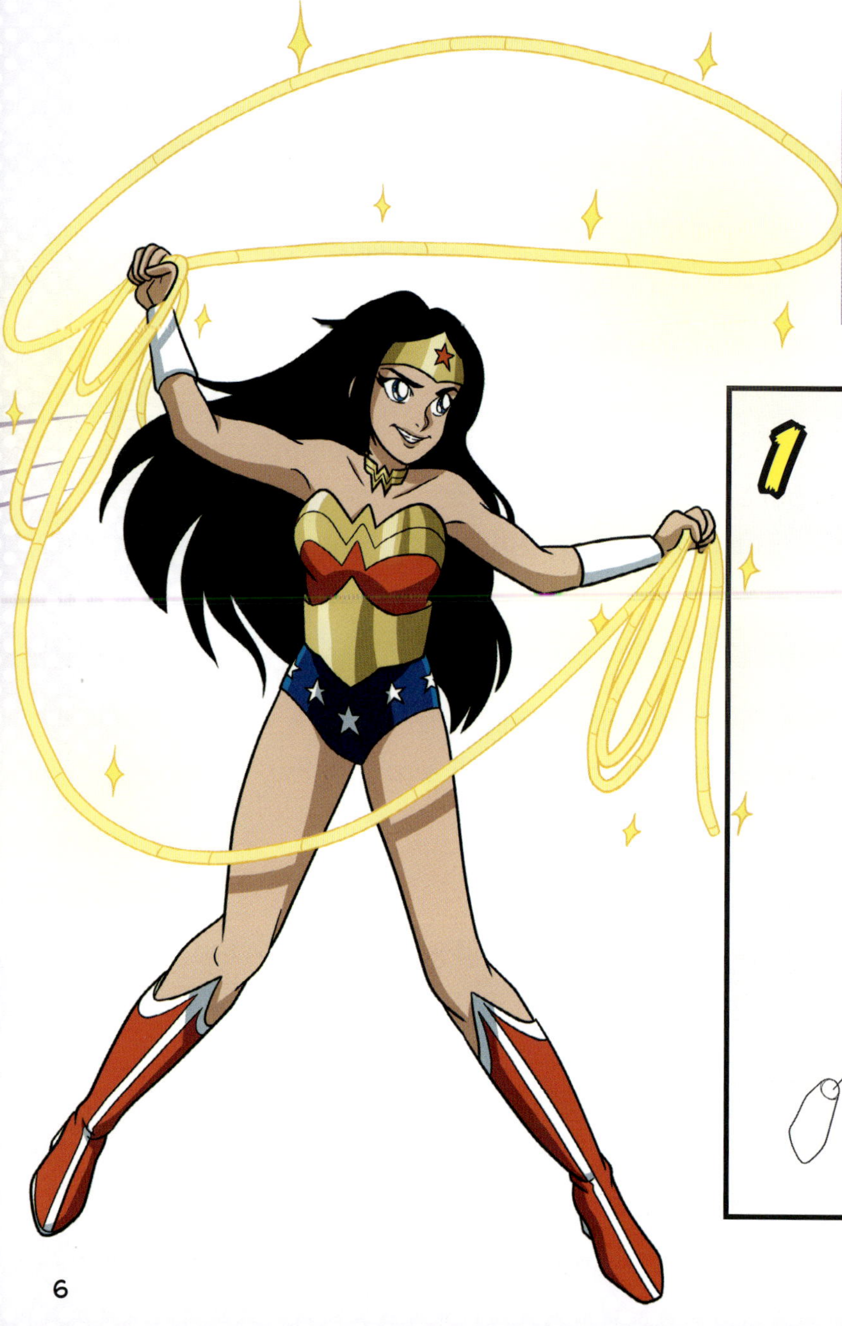

MANGA FACT

Manga is read right to left instead of left to right. Each page starts in the top right-hand corner, then goes panel to panel to finish at the bottom left-hand corner.

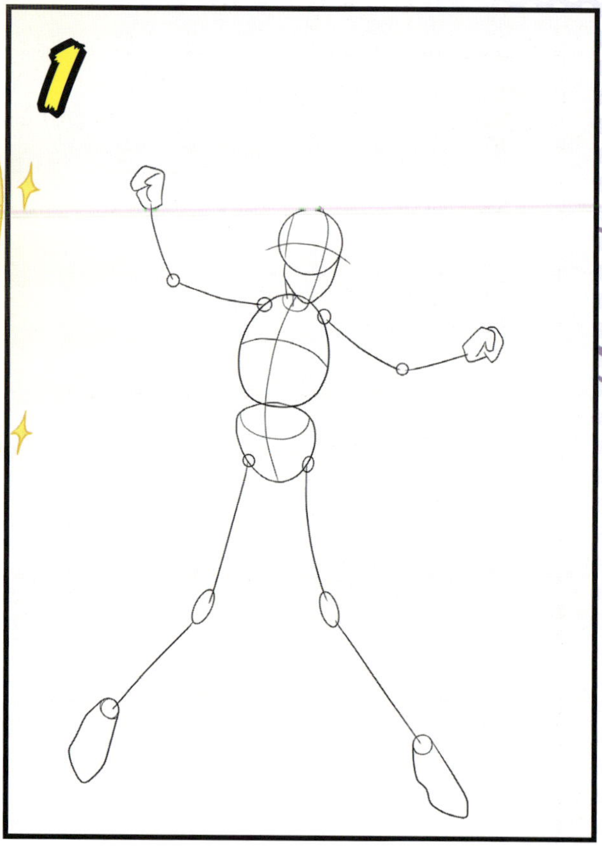
1

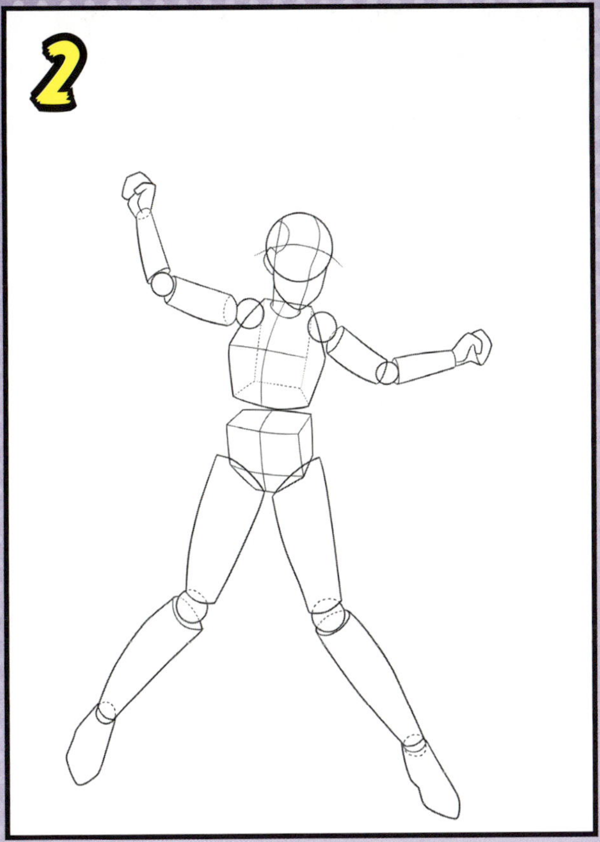
2
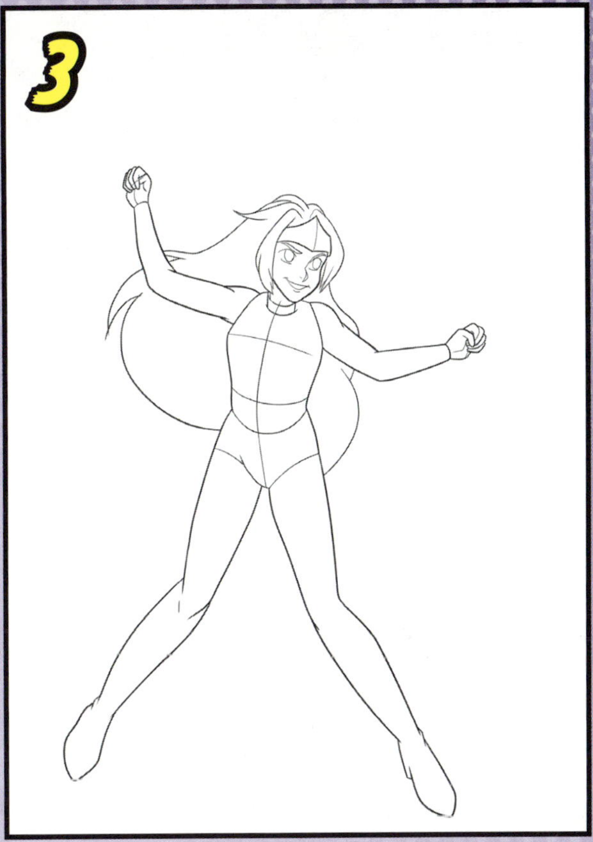
3
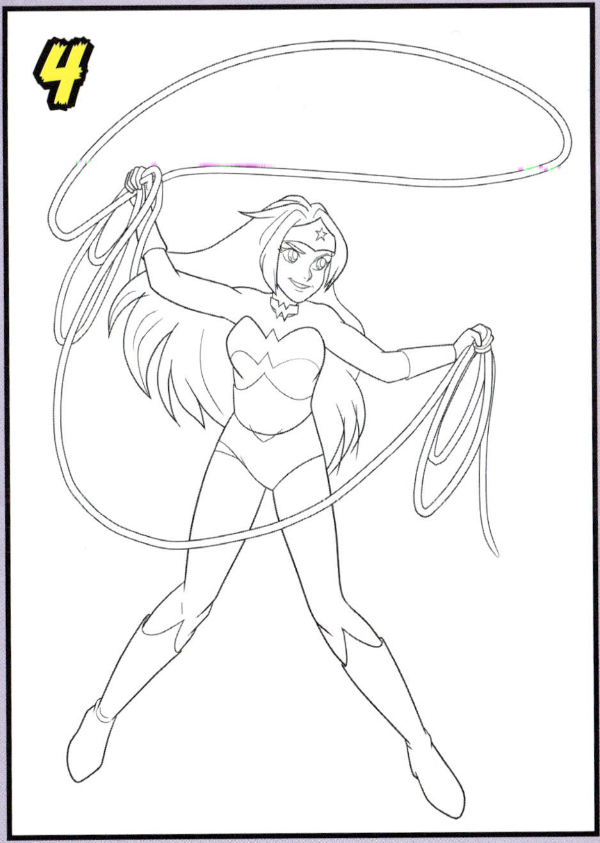
4
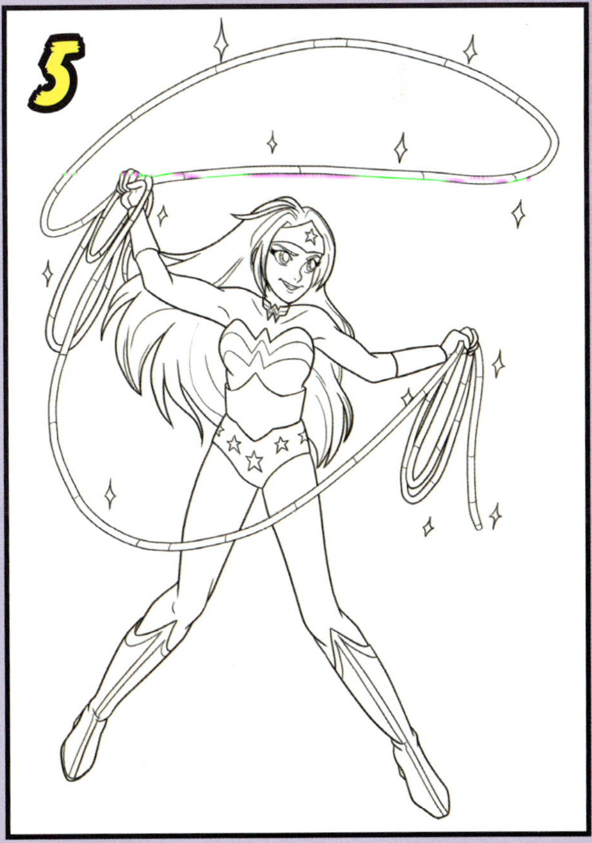
5

STEVE TREVOR

Every Super Hero benefits from a little backup. Luckily, Wonder Woman has Steve Trevor on her side. Not only is Trevor one of the Amazon warrior's most trusted friends, but he's also an agent of A.R.G.U.S. (Advanced Research Group Uniting Super-Humans). As a man with a plan and an appetite for action, Trevor is always ready to take a swing at crime.

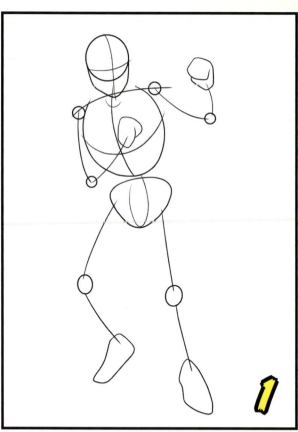

1

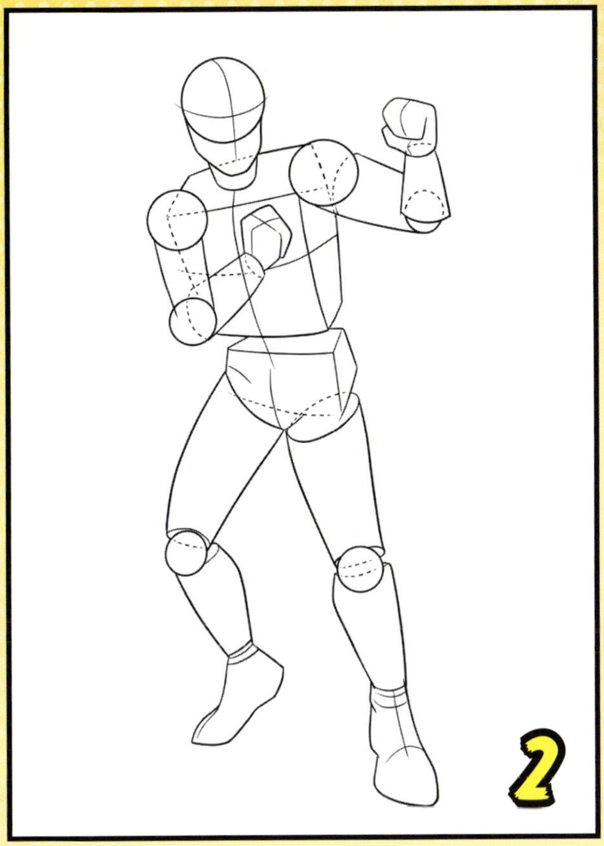
2
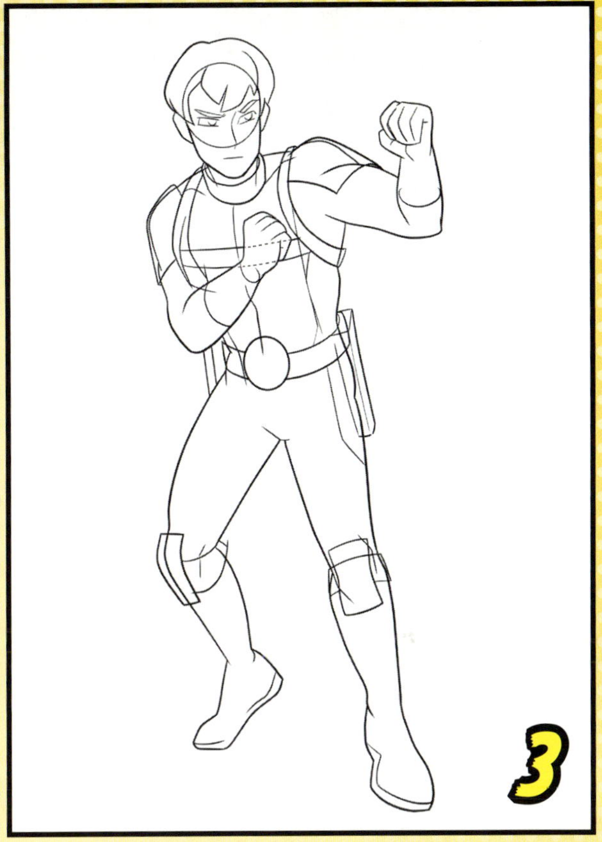
3
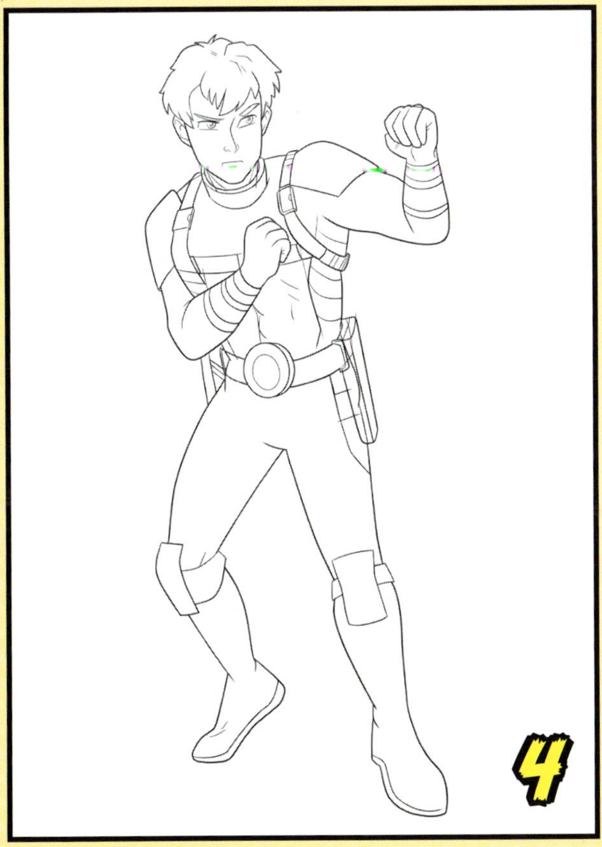
4
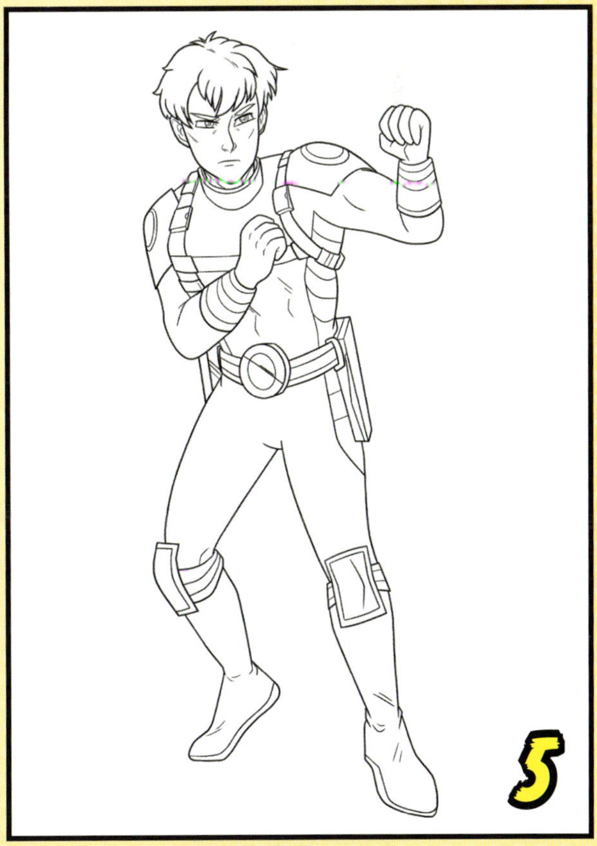
5

ETTA CANDY

A.R.G.U.S. agent Etta Candy's sweet spot is saving the day alongside Wonder Woman. The bold and bubbly intelligence officer is just as happy decoding data as she is bounding into battle. Whenever Princess Diana gets in a bind, Etta comes in to kick things up a notch!

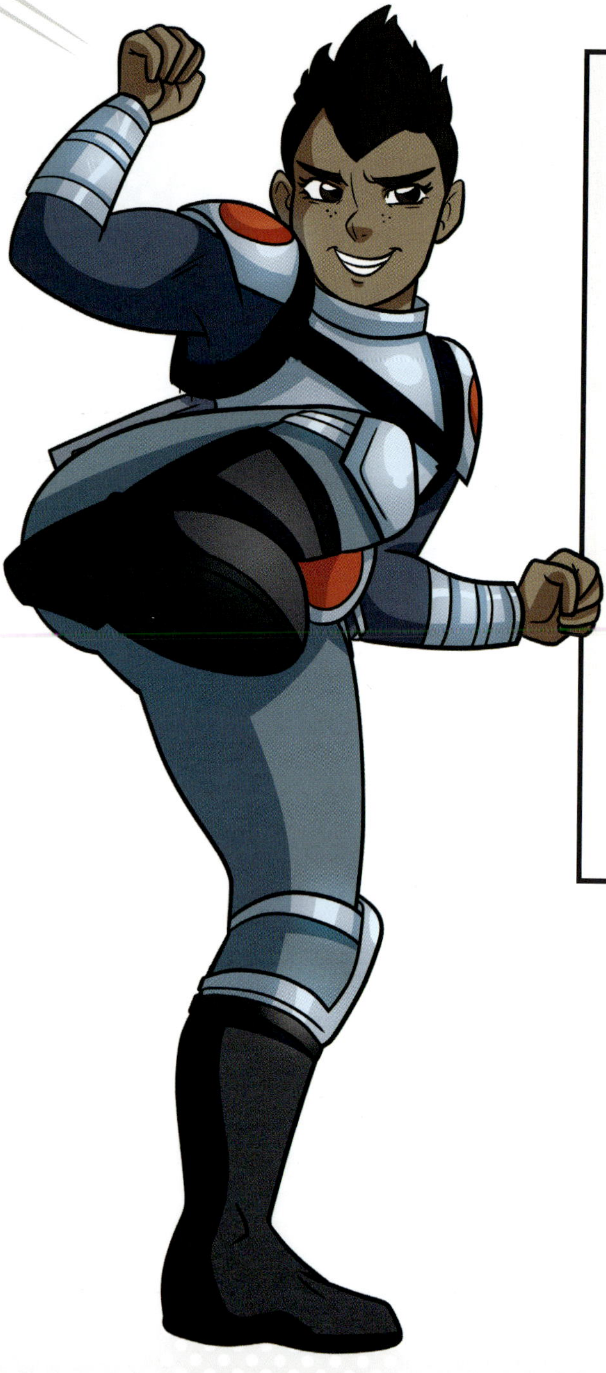

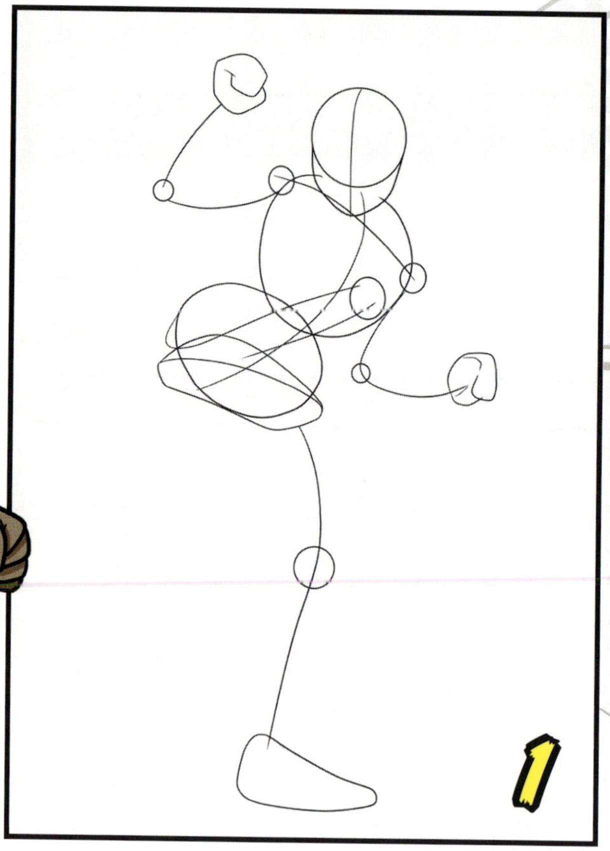
1

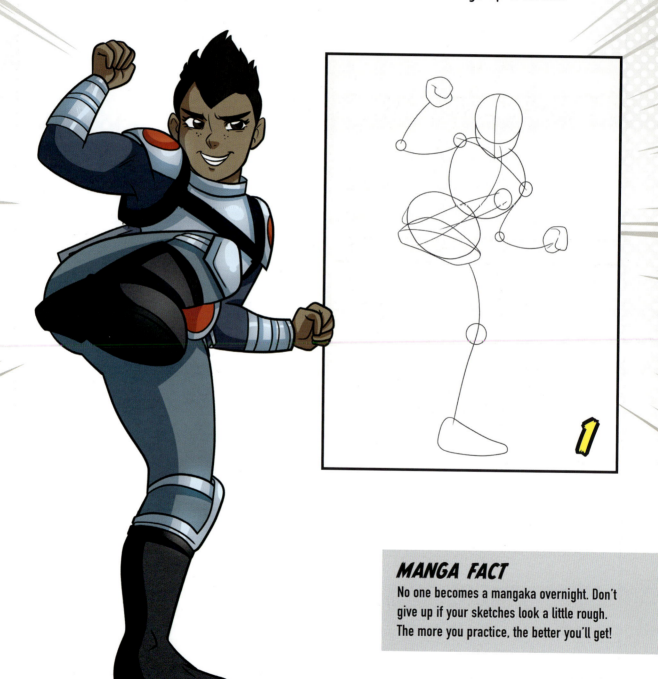

MANGA FACT

No one becomes a mangaka overnight. Don't give up if your sketches look a little rough. The more you practice, the better you'll get!

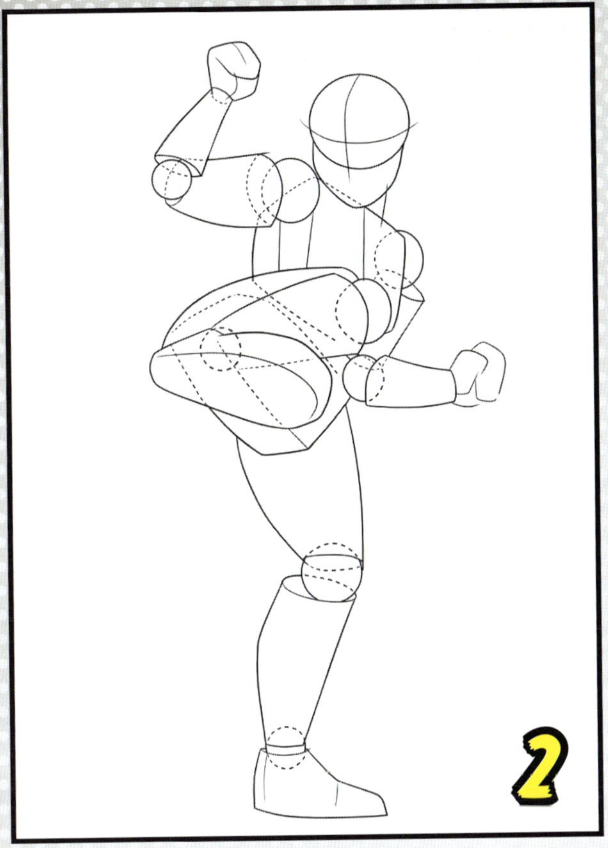
2
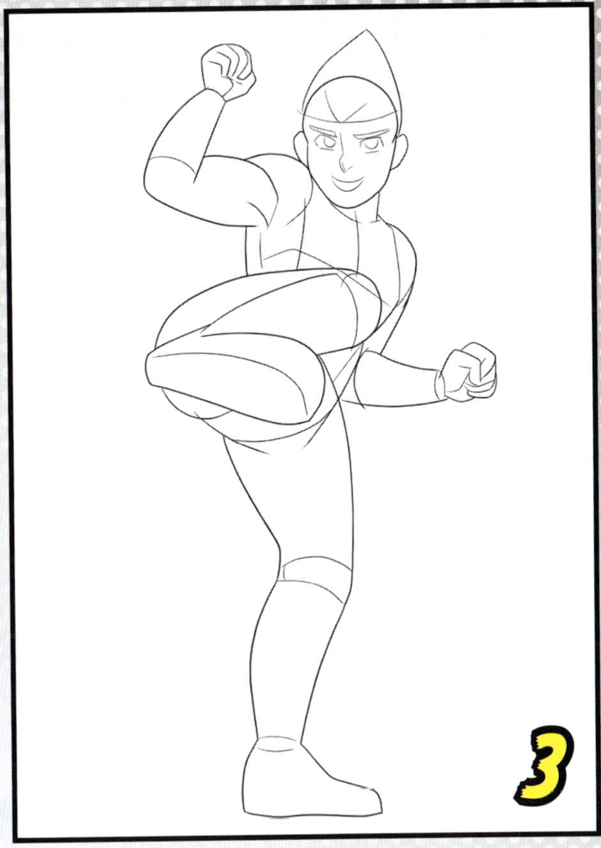
3
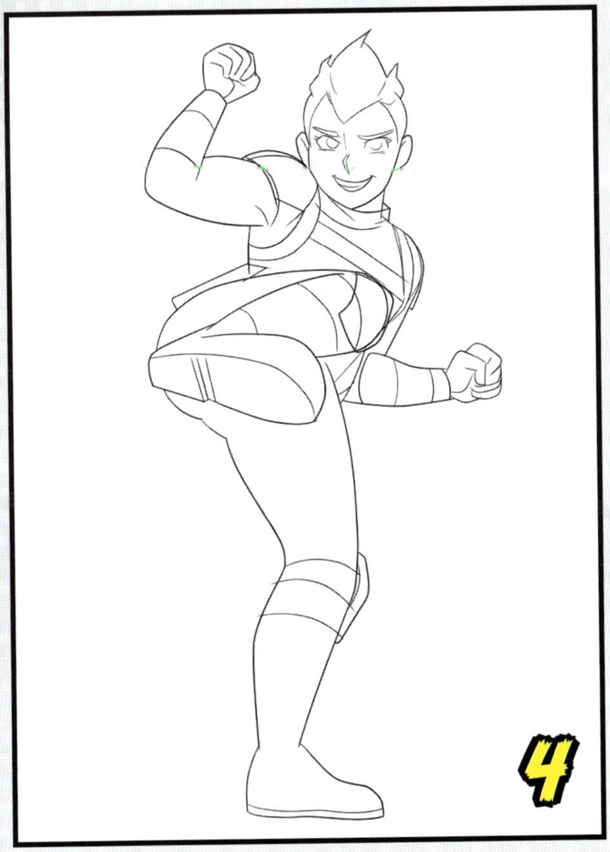
4
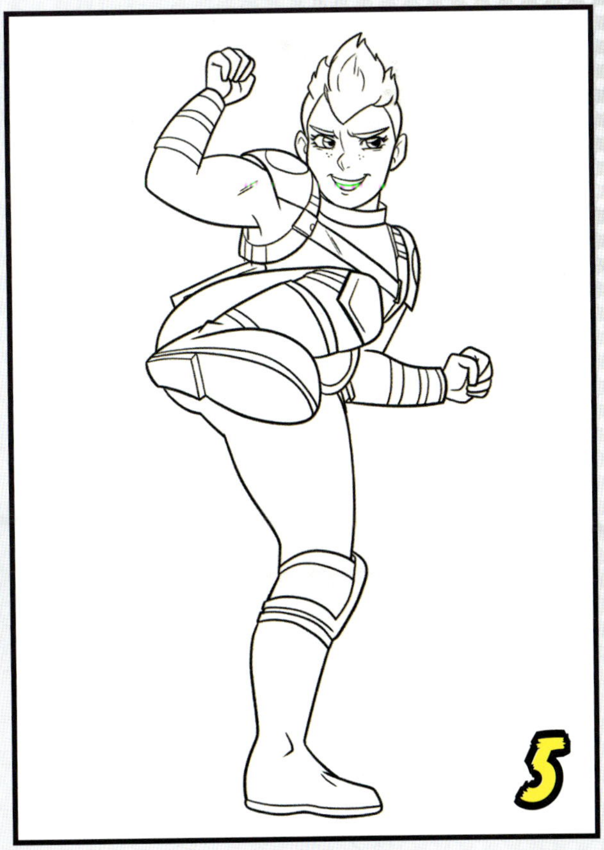
5

QUEEN HIPPOLYTA

All hail Queen Hippolyta! She is the wise ruler of the island of Themyscira, the fierce leader of the Amazons . . . and a marvelous mother. Long ago Hippolyta was blessed by the gods with a daughter, Diana. With such a majestic mom, it's no wonder Princess Diana grew up to become Wonder Woman!

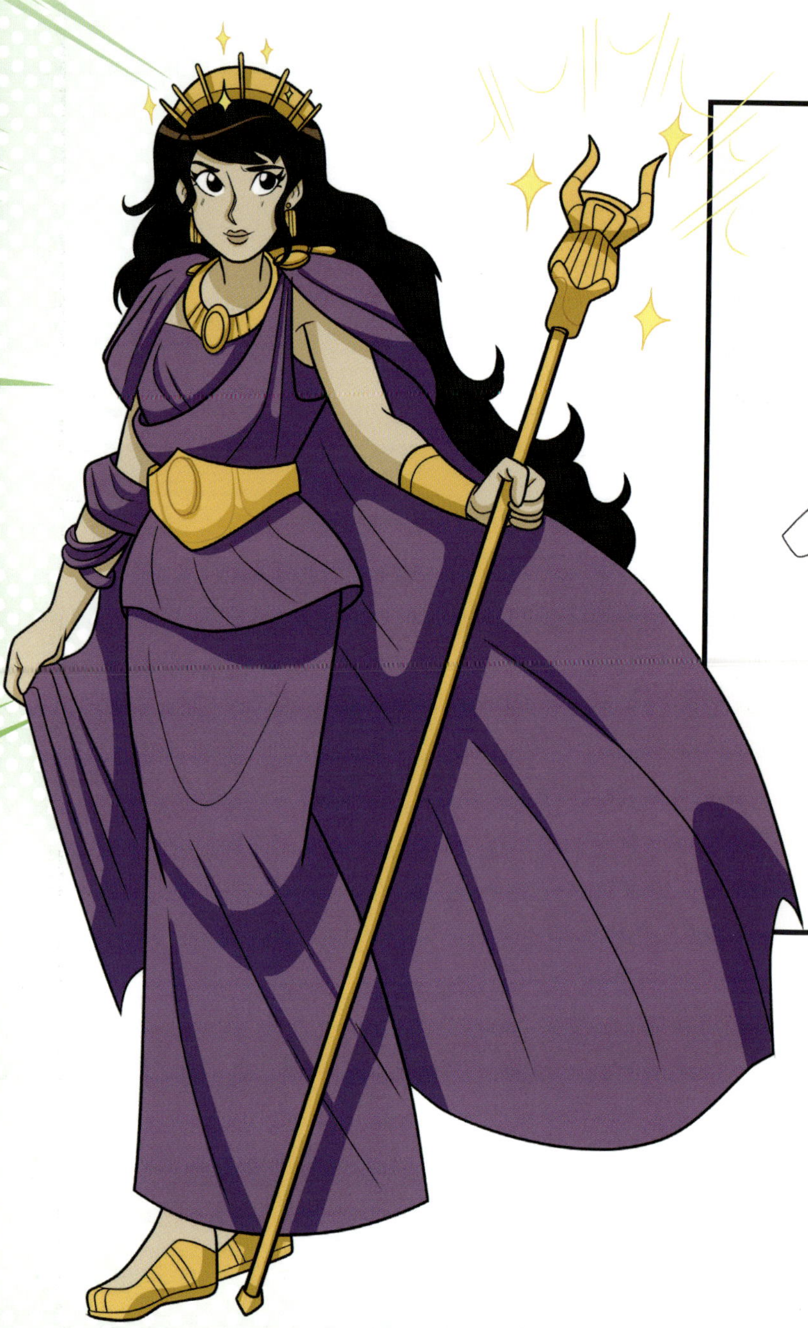

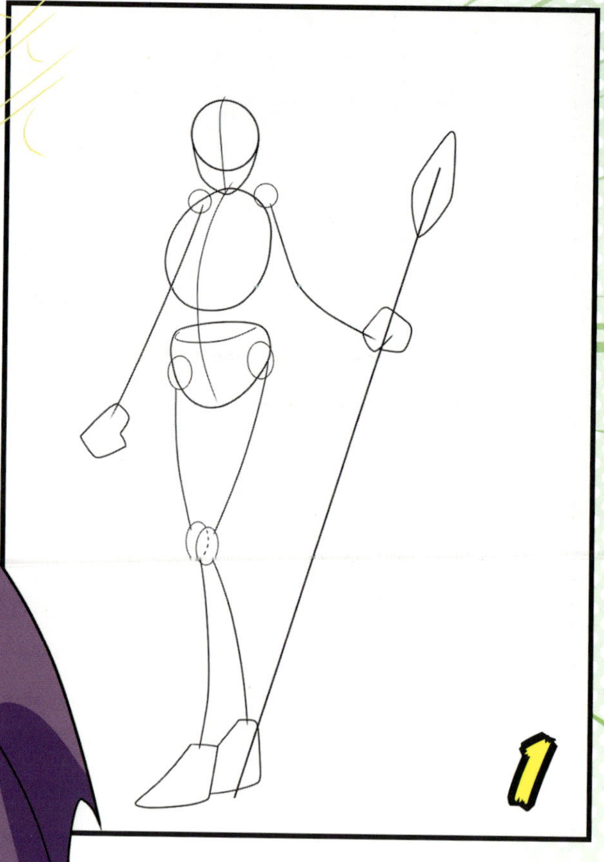
1

MANGA FACT

Manga characters may have over-the-top features, but they're often based on real life. Want to change up a pose? Look at photos of people to help you nail a new look.

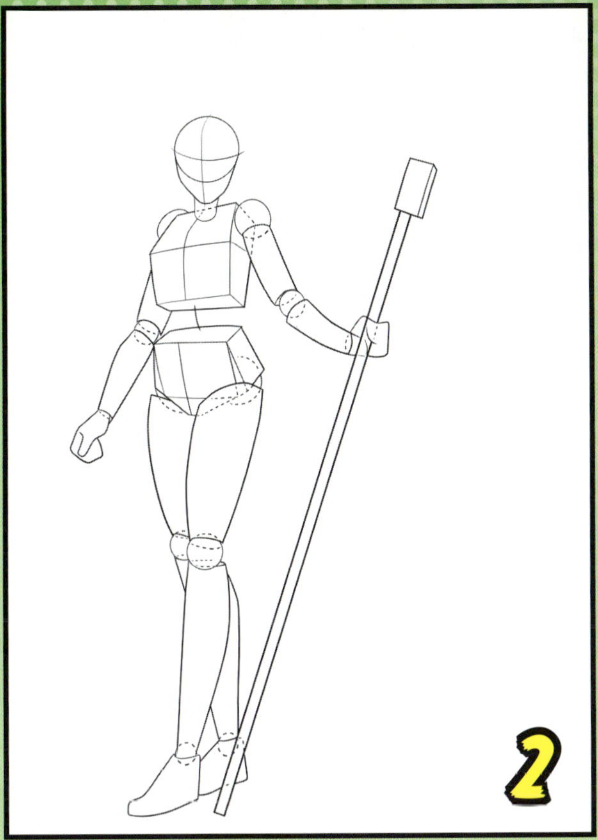
2
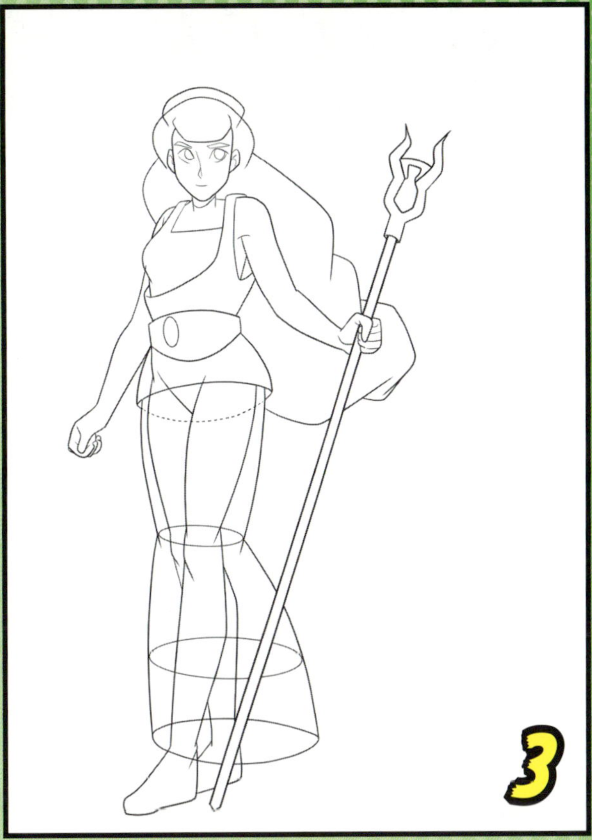
3
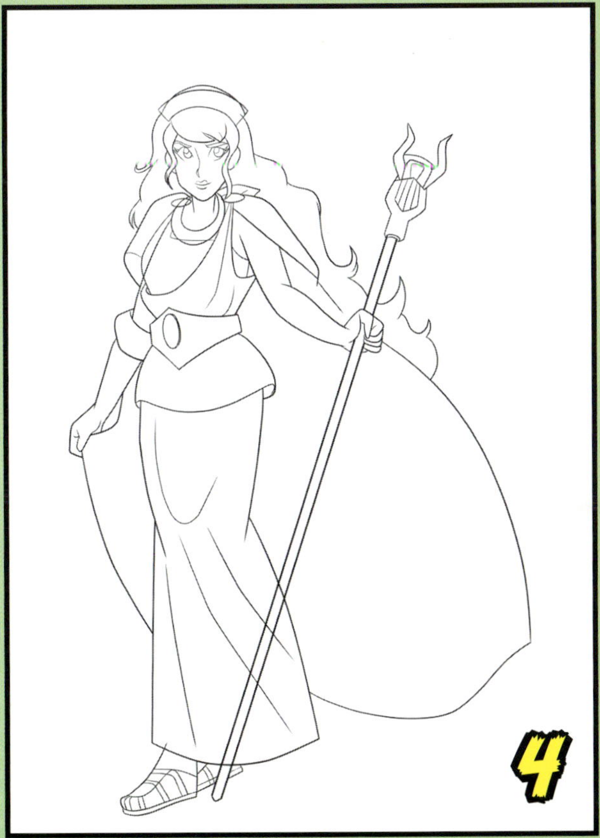
4
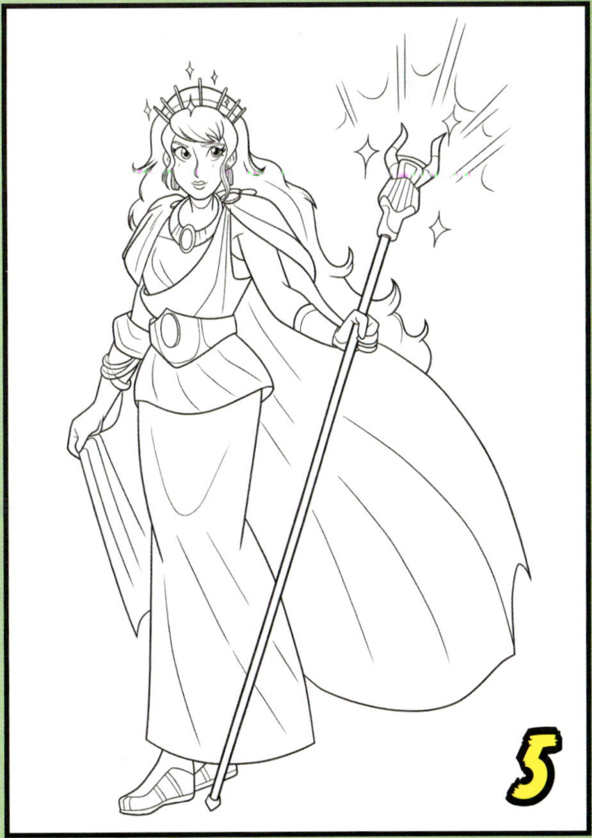
5

PHILIPPUS

When Wonder Woman wanted to learn the ways of the warrior, she turned to Philippus. It'd be hard to find a better teacher. The immortal Amazon general has more than 3,000 years of battle experience! She's not afraid to enter the fray. She skillfully fends off foes with a flurry of her fists or a slash of her sword!

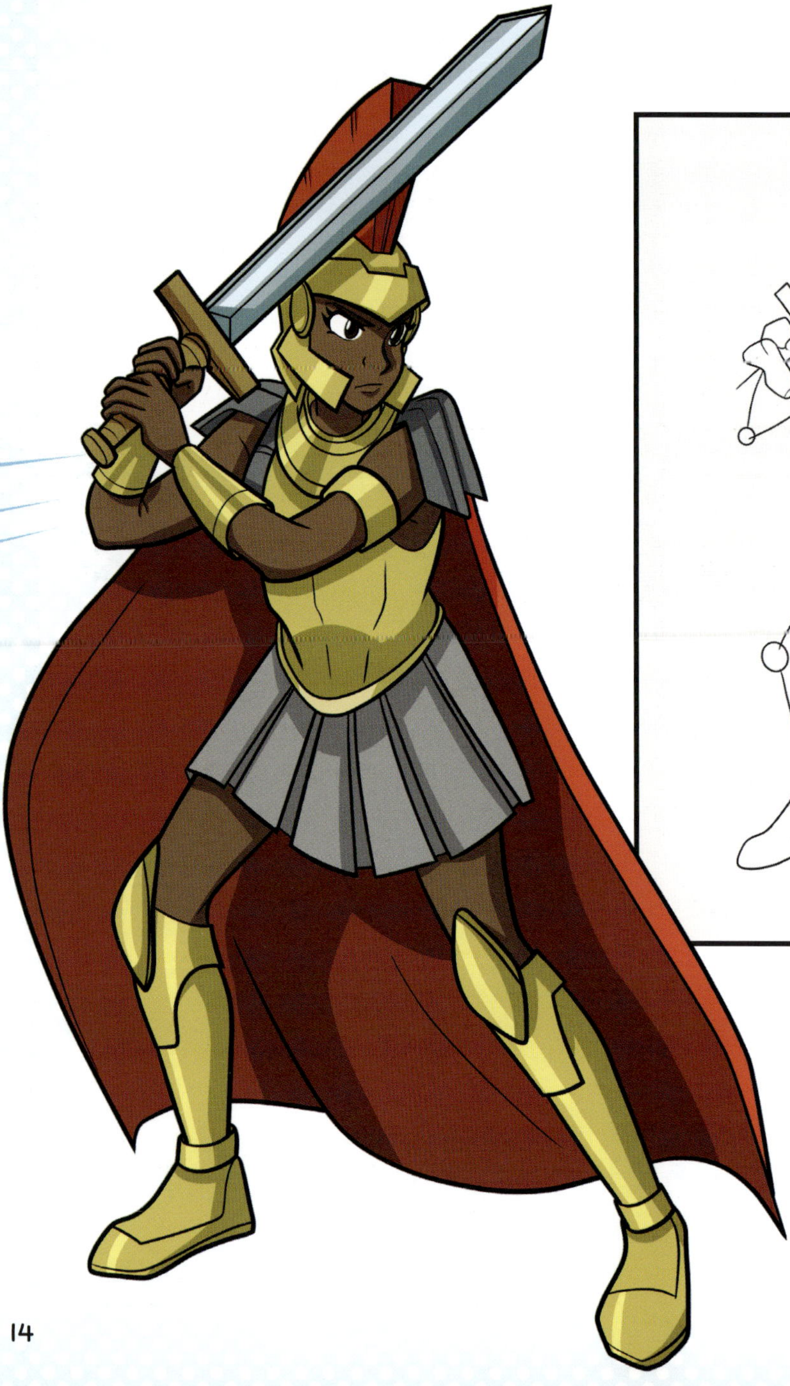

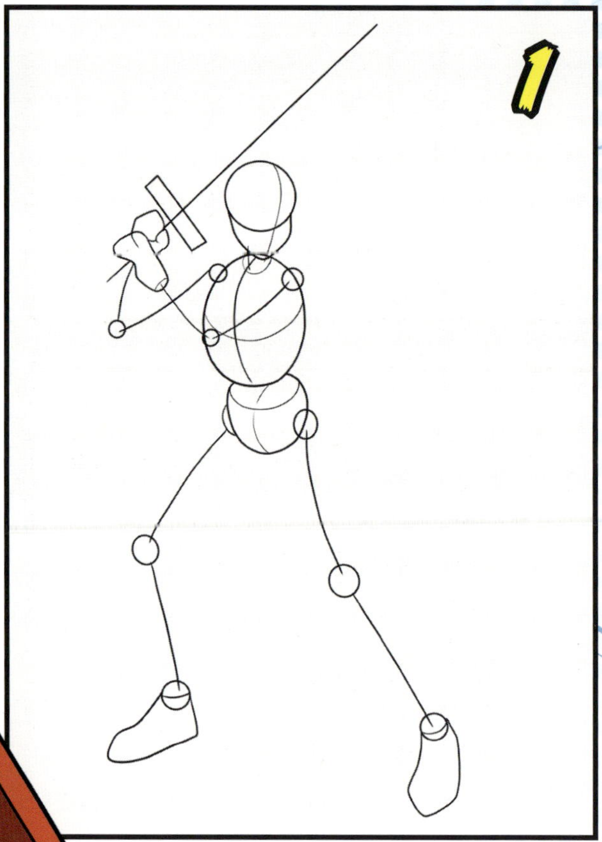
1

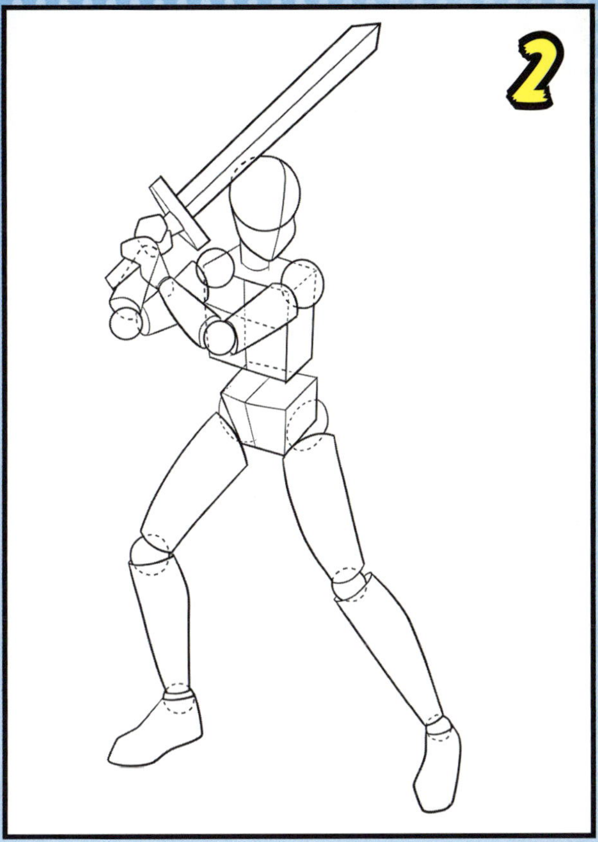
2
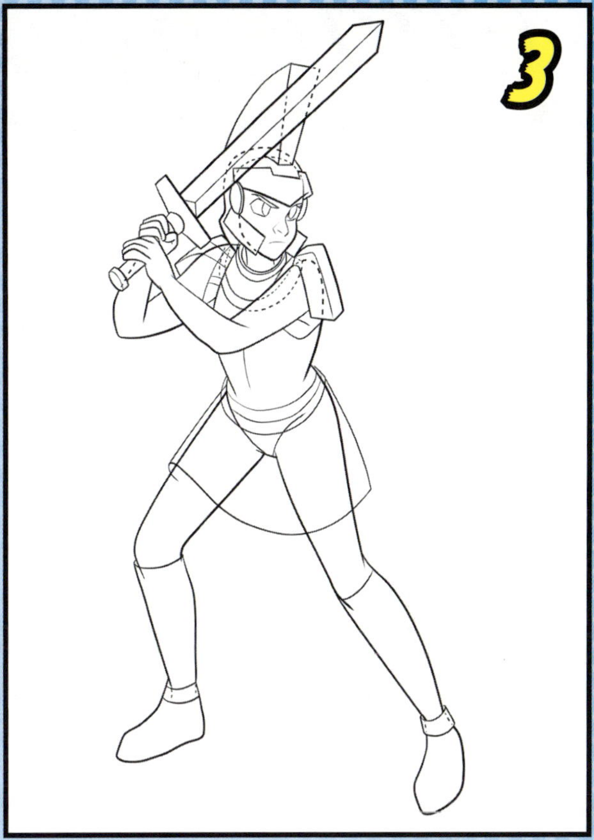
3
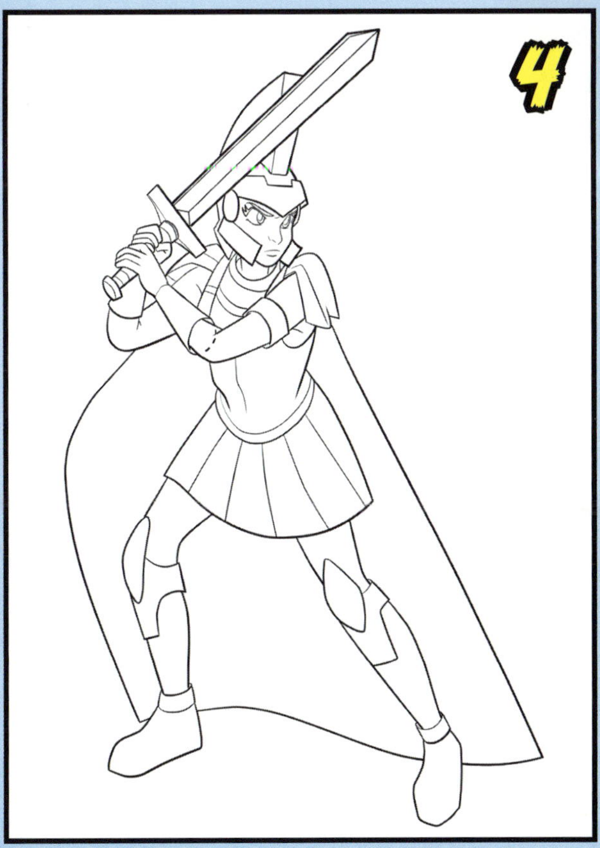
4
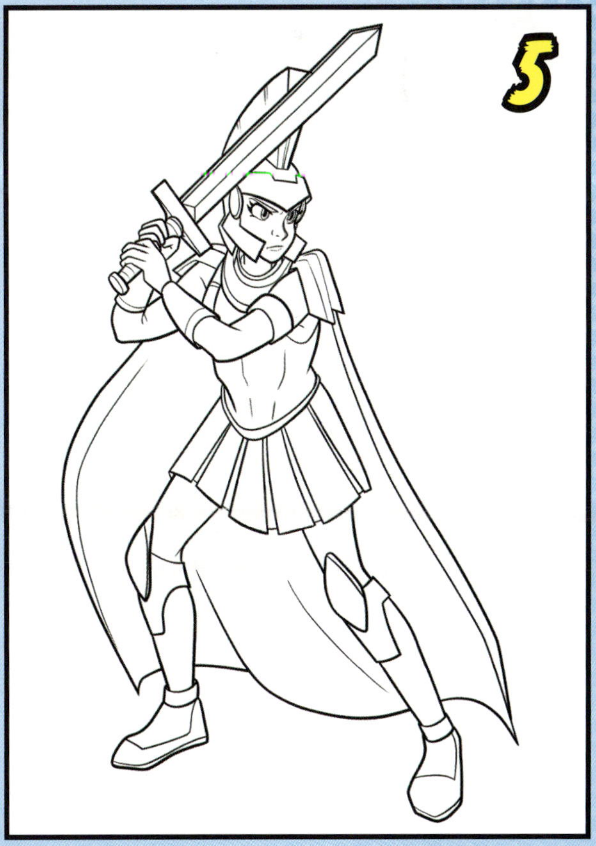
5

THE CHEETAH

Watch out! The Cheetah is on the prowl! This scientist-turned-Super-Villain is a *fur*-ocious fighter. She sports catlike agility, beastly strength, and razor-sharp claws that are capable of slashing straight through solid stone. The Cheetah will never *paws* while taking a swipe at Wonder Woman!

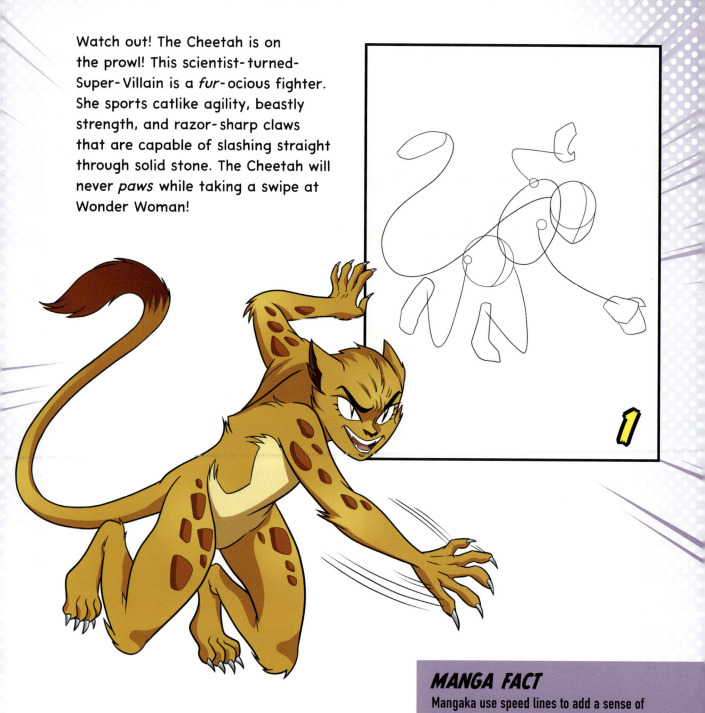

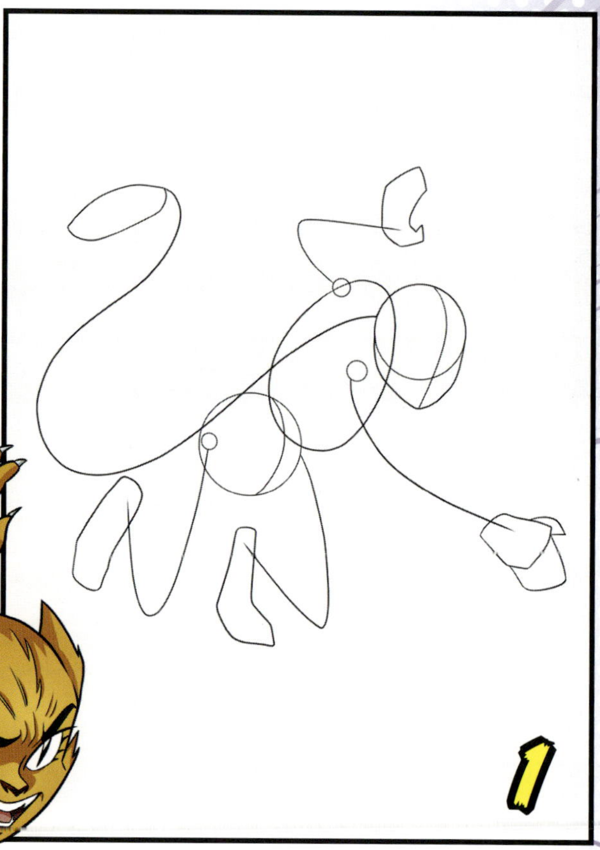
1

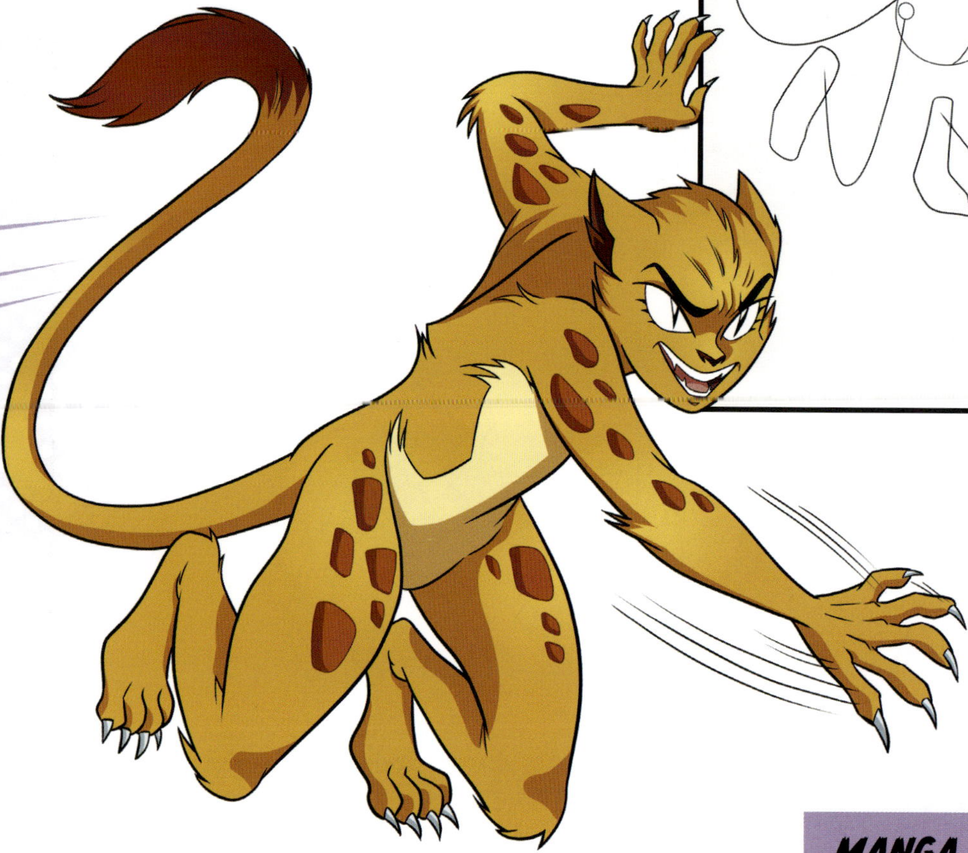

MANGA FACT

Mangaka use speed lines to add a sense of motion. Draw a burst of speed lines around The Cheetah to help her leap off the page!

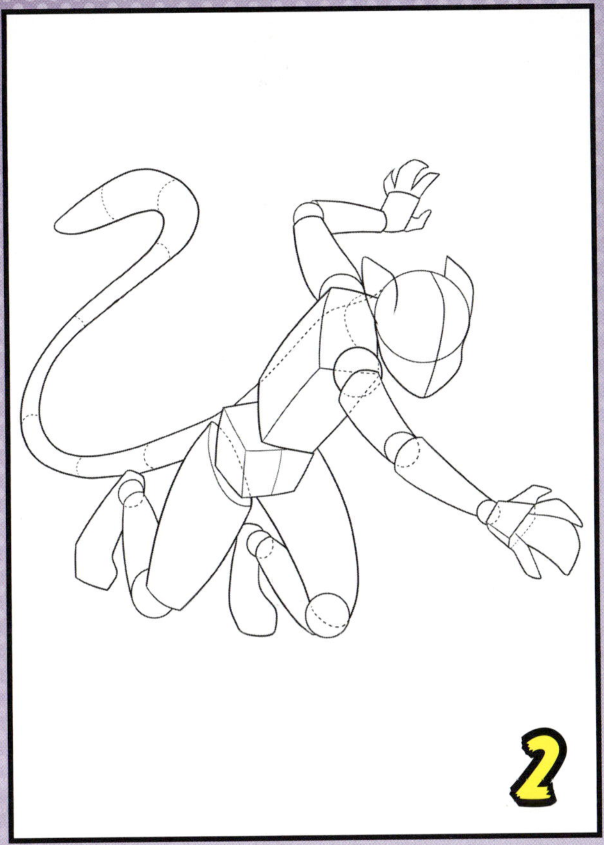
2

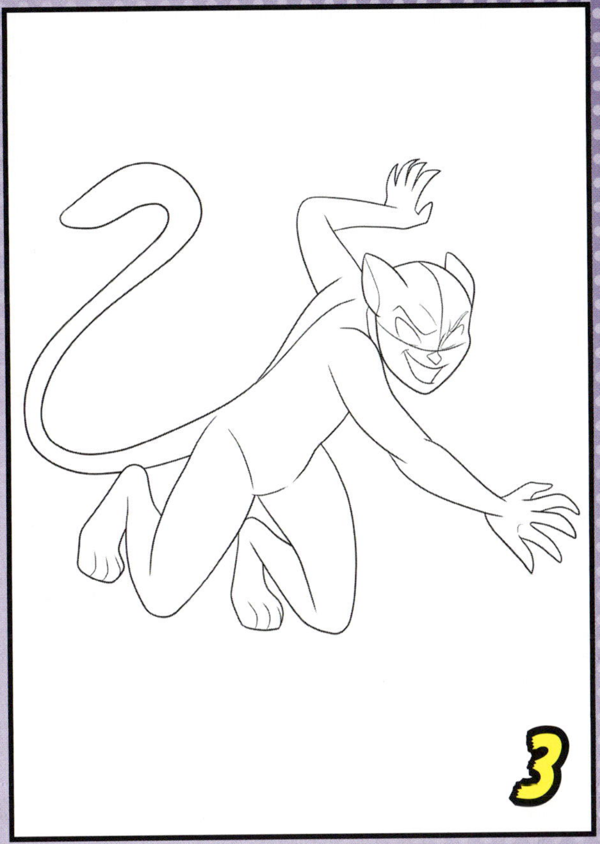
3

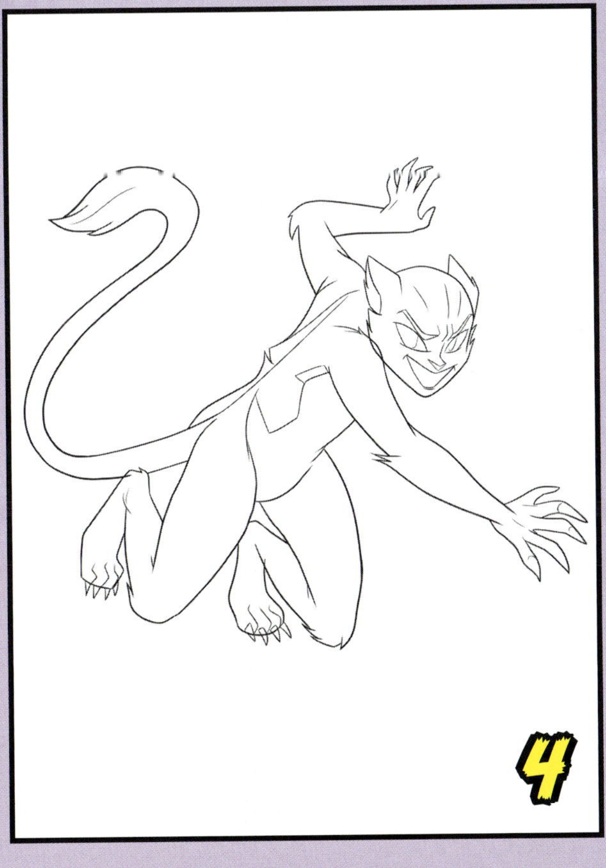
4

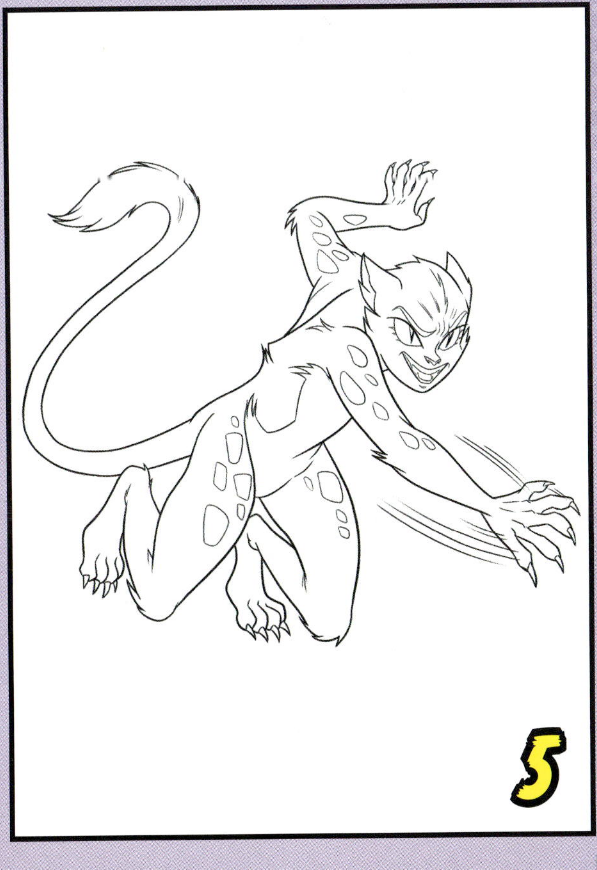
5

ARES

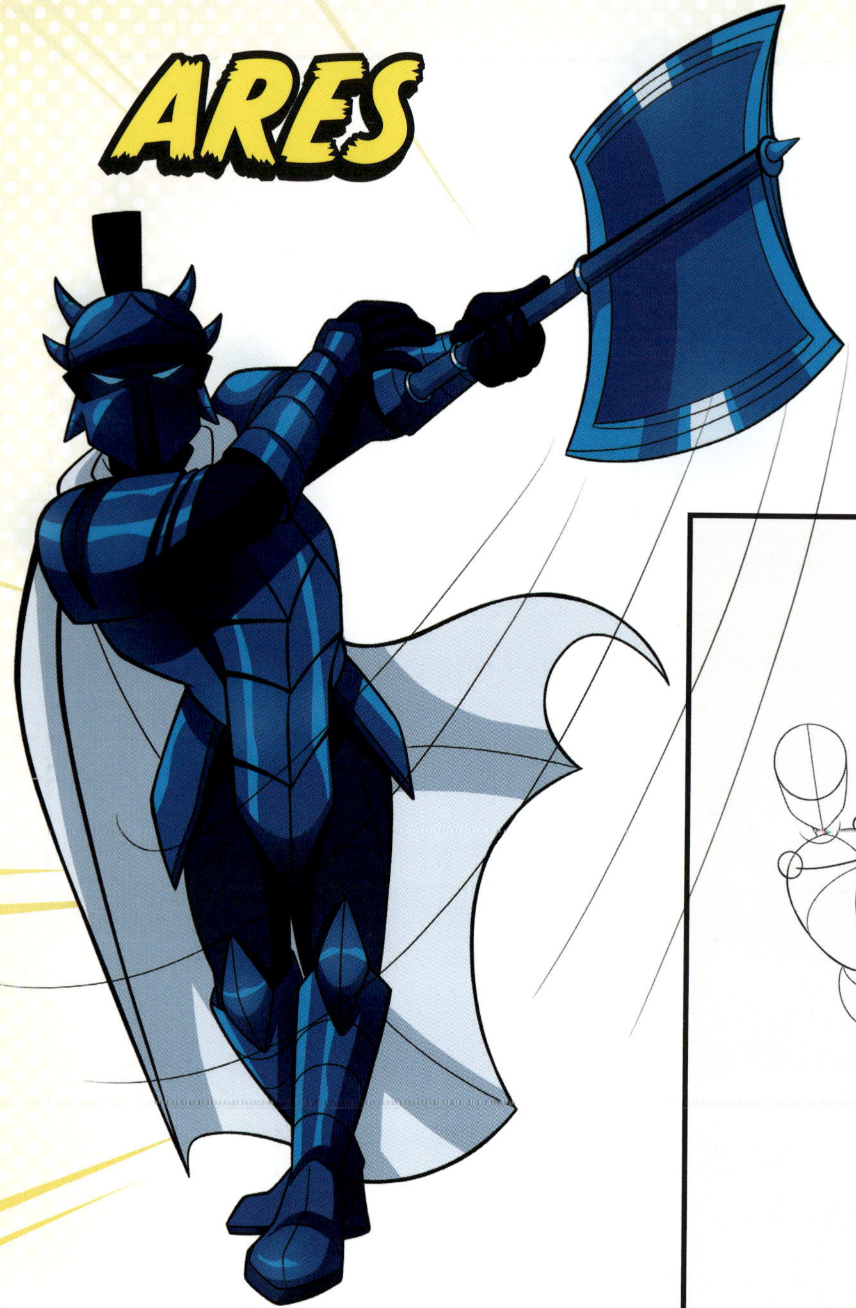

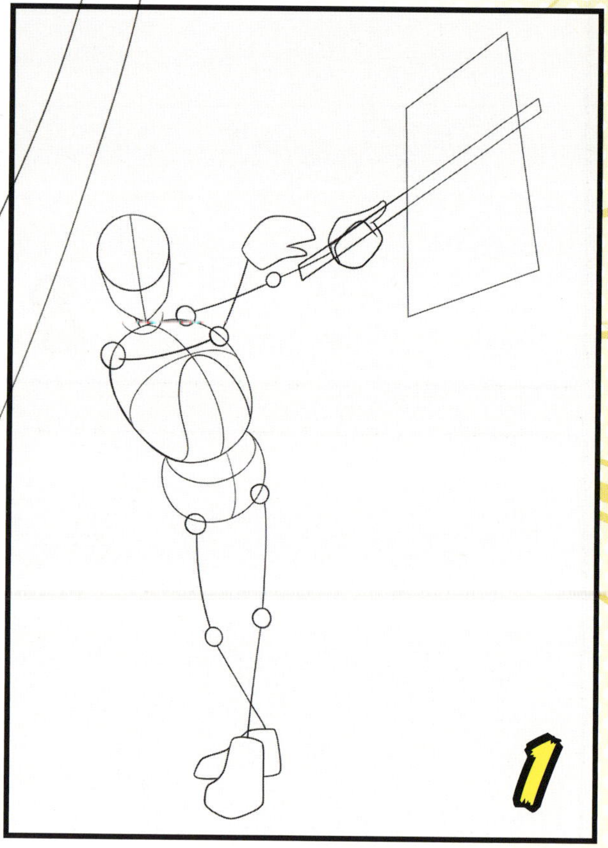
1

Ares always has an axe to grind. As the Greek god of war, he tricks mortals into fighting among themselves. And the more hate he creates, the more powerful he becomes. From superhuman strength and indestructibility to shape-shifting and teleportation, this malicious immortal has the means to make massive mayhem!

MANGA FACT

The chibi style makes even sinister characters cute! Try drawing Ares as a chibi with a tiny body and large head.

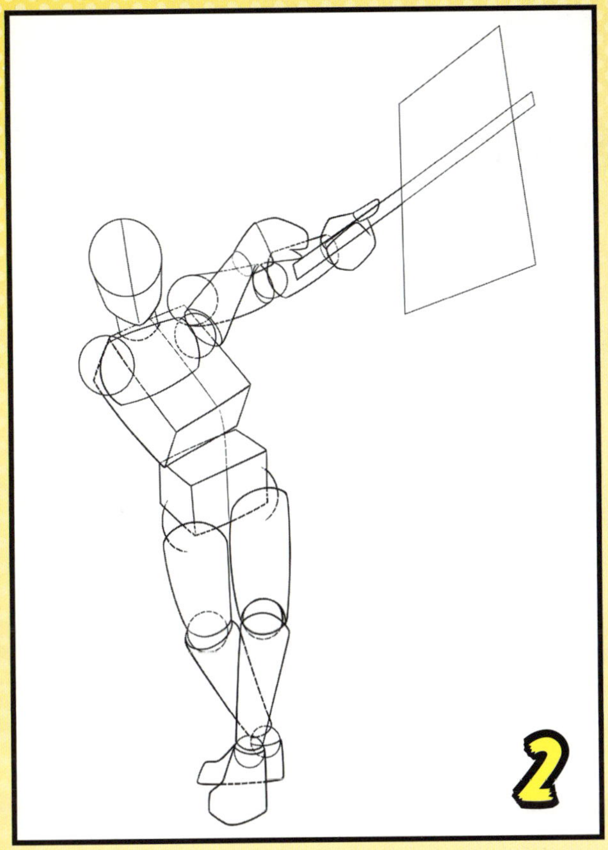
2
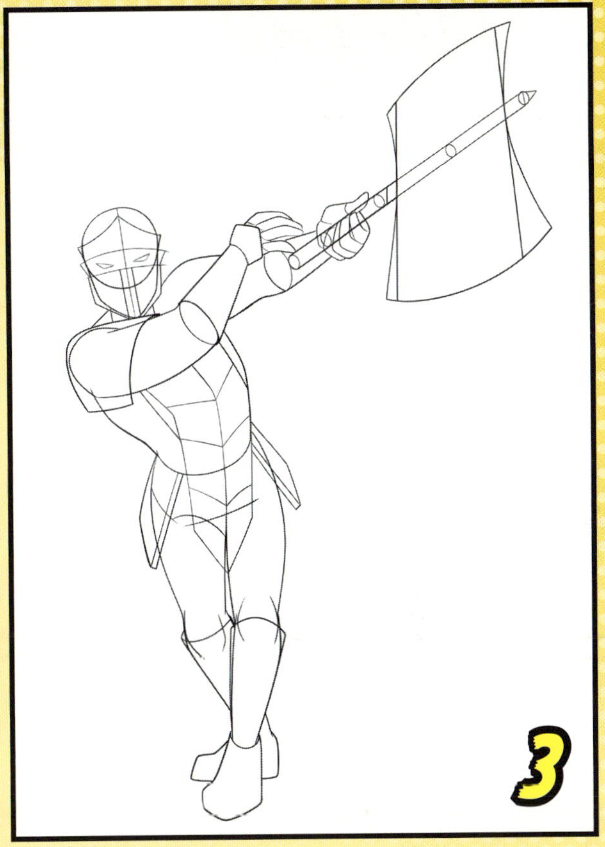
3
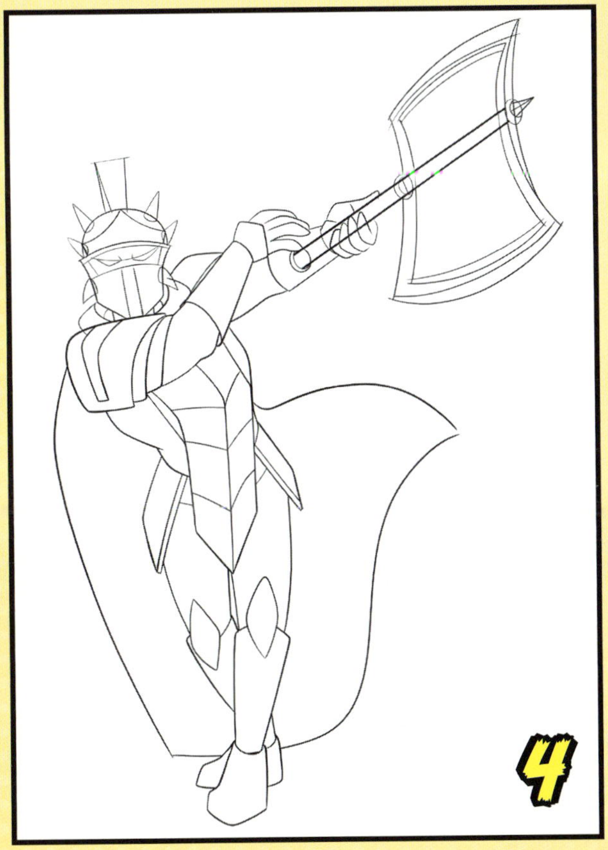
4
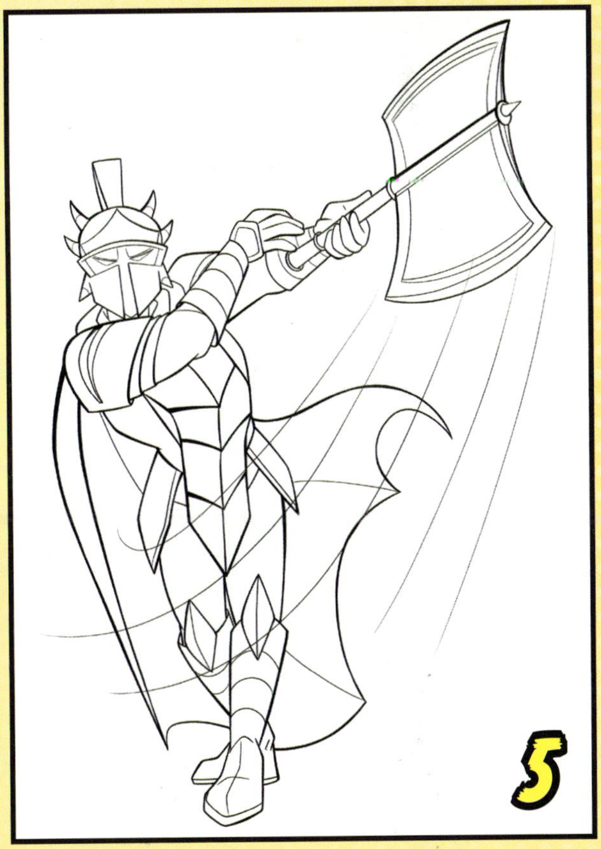
5

The sorceress Circe has a mischievous mission: Make life difficult for Wonder Woman. Using mind-bending spells, she can create evil illusions and teleport anywhere in the world. On top of that, Circe never gets *boared* of her signature move—turning opponents into pigs!

MANGA FACT
A manga character's eye shape can say a lot about how they feel. Experiment with the shape of Circe's eyes and eyebrows to show different emotions.

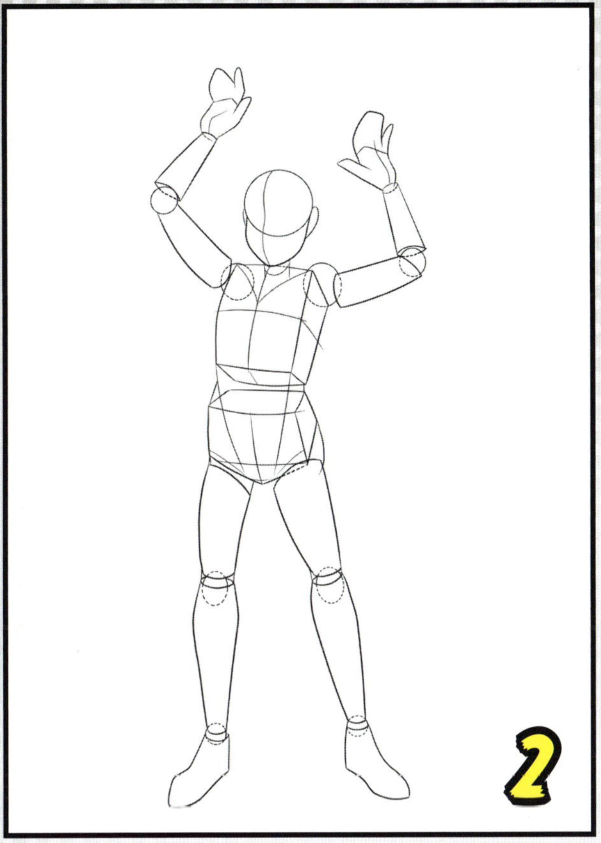
2
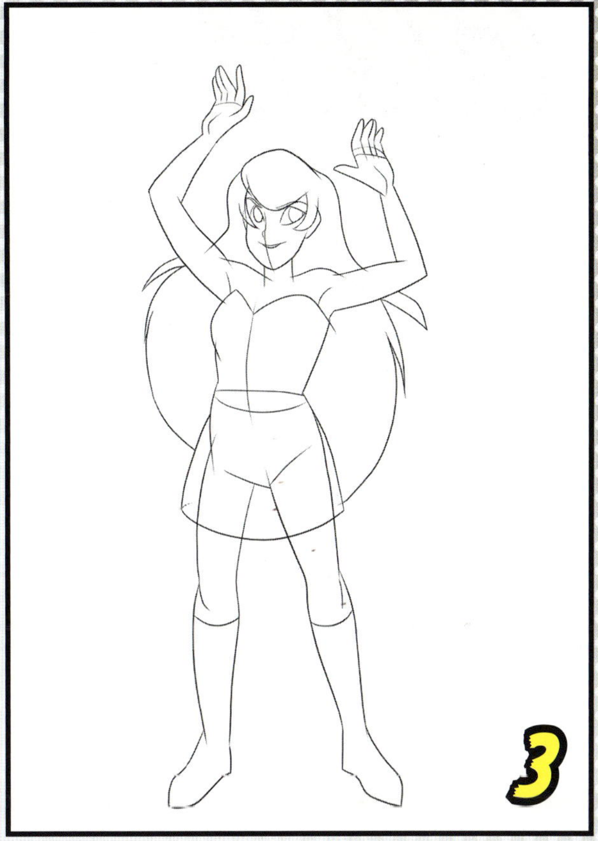
3
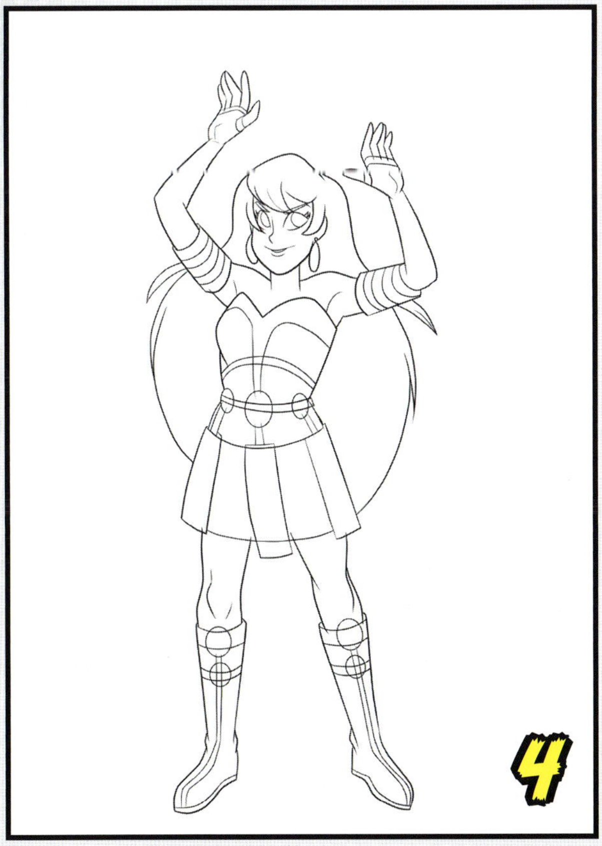
4
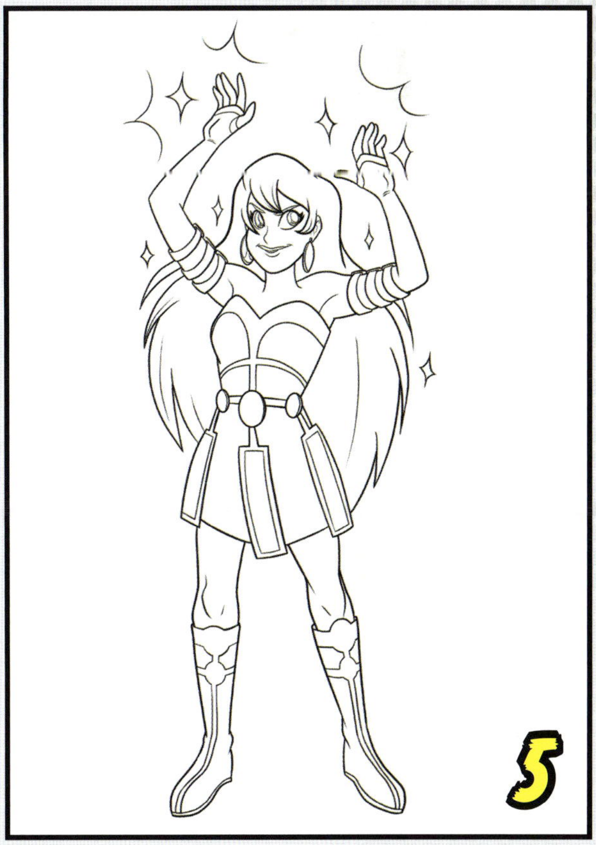
5

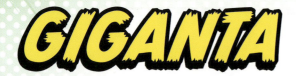

GIGANTA

It's fair to say Giganta stands head and shoulders above other crooks. The size-shifting Super-Villain can grow from normal human height into a towering titan in no time flat! And her might multiplies as she gets bigger. At her largest, Giganta is stronger than Wonder Woman and can crush anything she clutches!

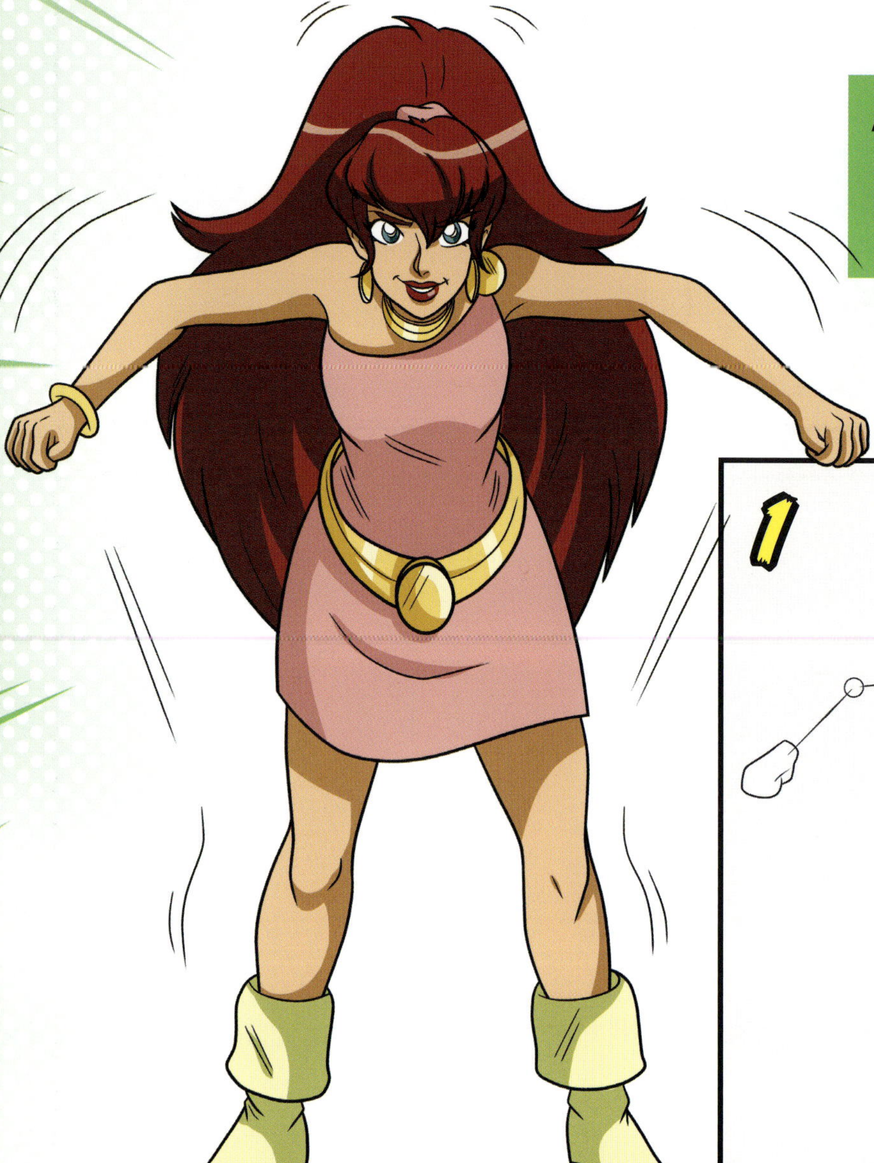

MANGA FACT

In 2021, Japan's manga industry took in more than $5 billion in sales of printed and digital materials!

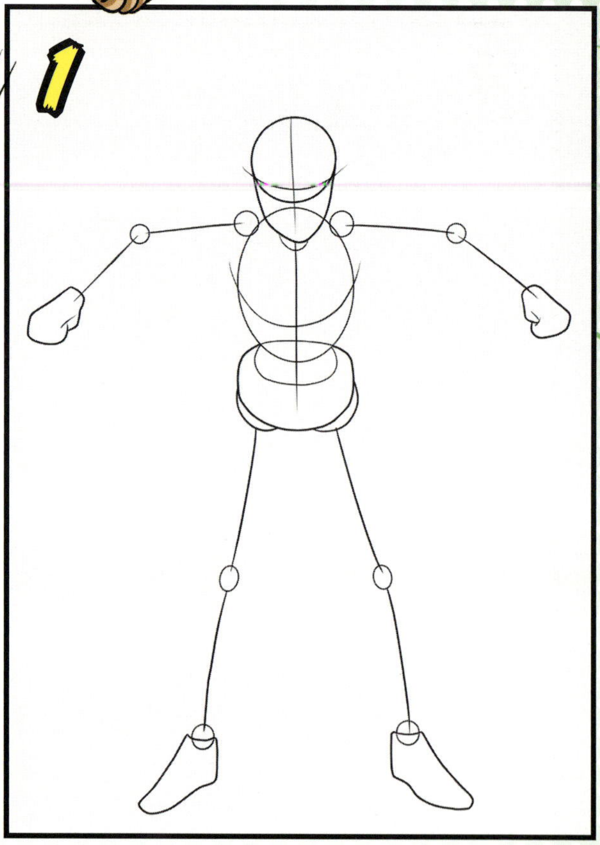
1

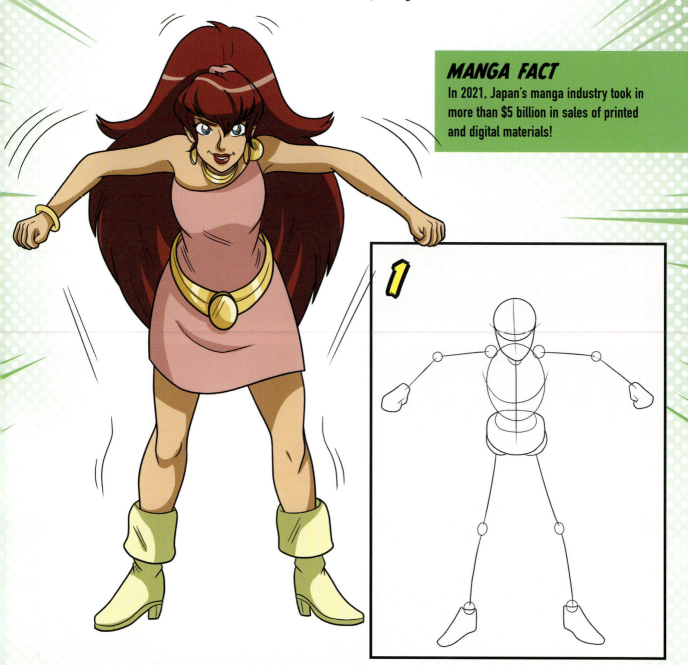

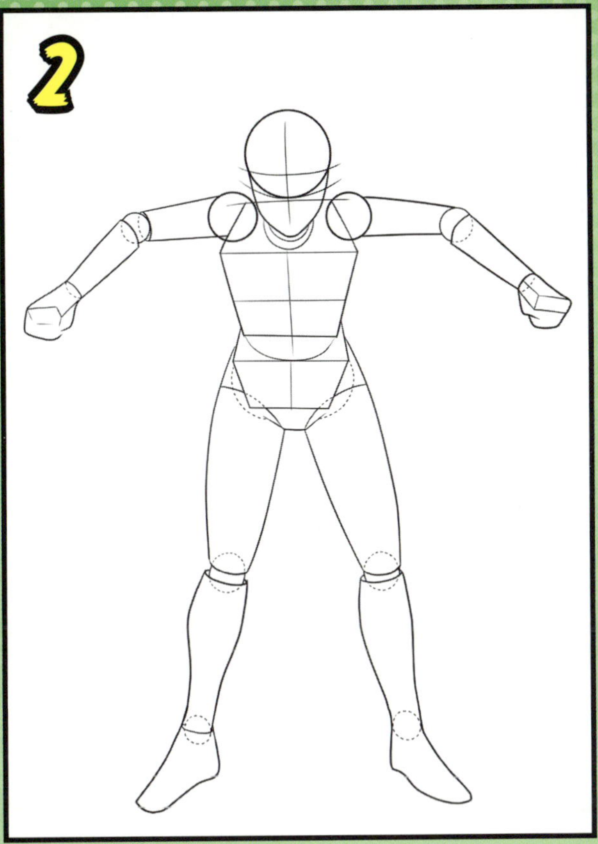
2
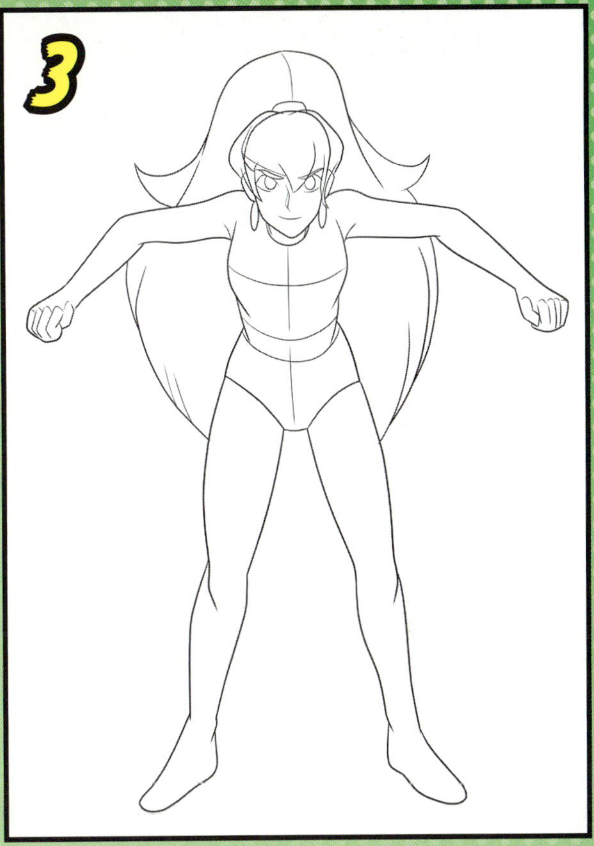
3
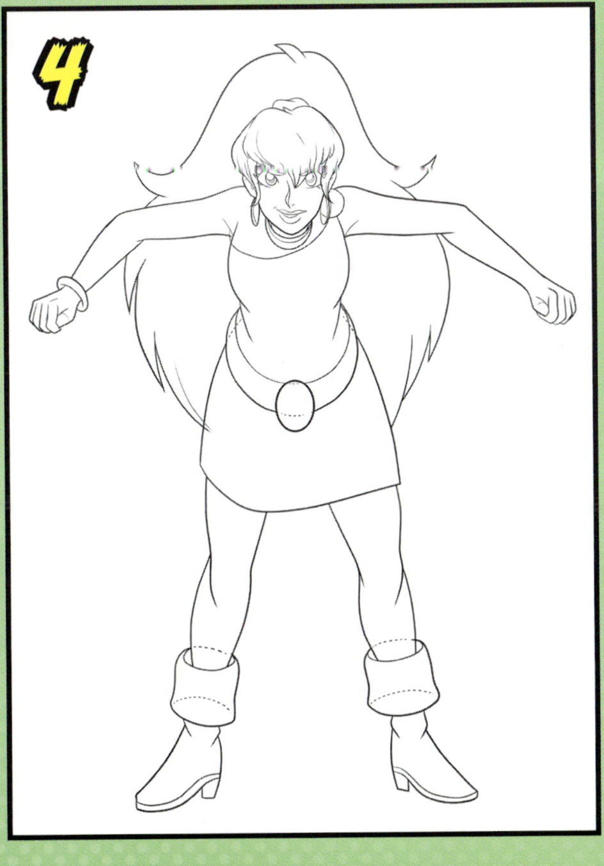
4
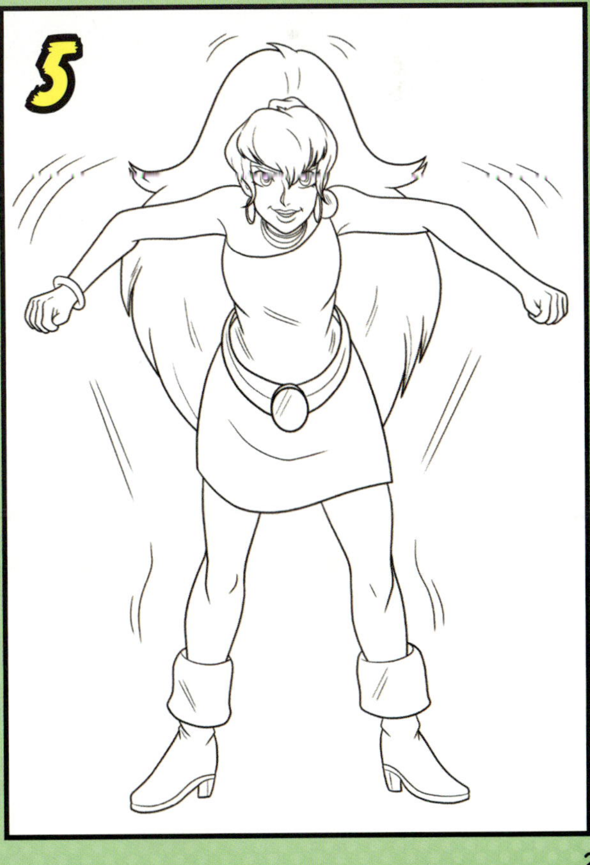
5

DEVASTATION

To defeat the Amazons, the Greek god Cronus decided to make a living weapon. Out of clay, he formed a twisted copy of Princess Diana. The result? A child named Devastation. With Wonder Woman's strength, durability, and speed, Devastation is determined to bend the Super Hero to her will!

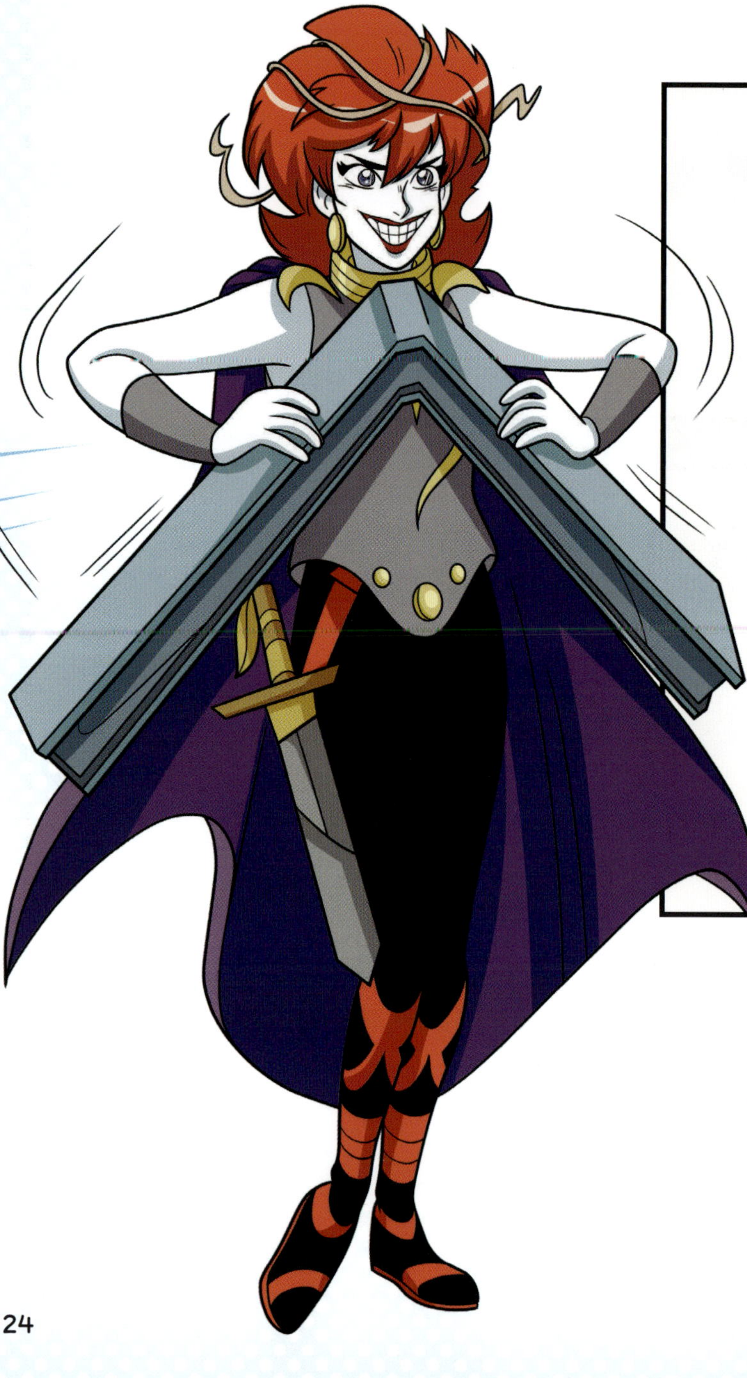

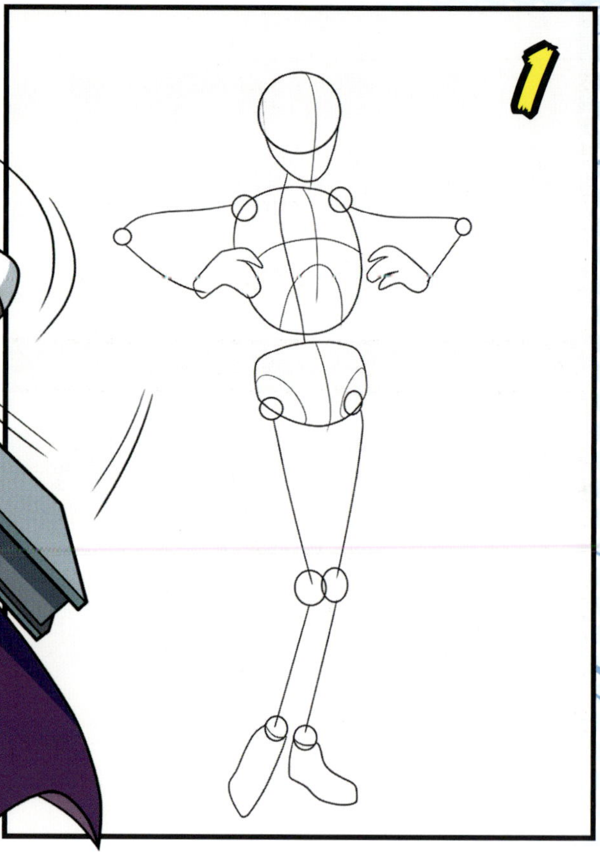
1

MANGA FACT

Manga and *anime* mean two different things. Anime is any animated story made in Japan. Manga is printed. But if a manga series is popular, it might be adapted into an anime.

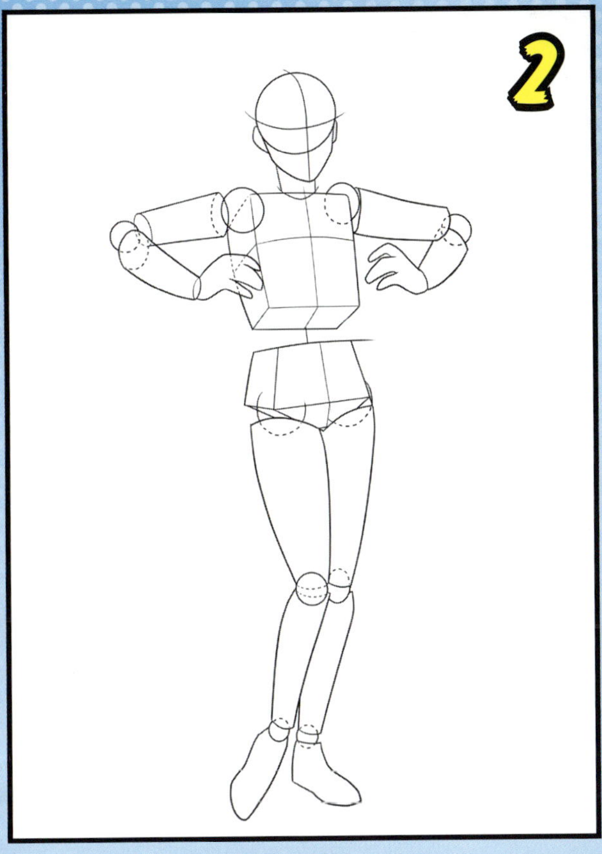
2
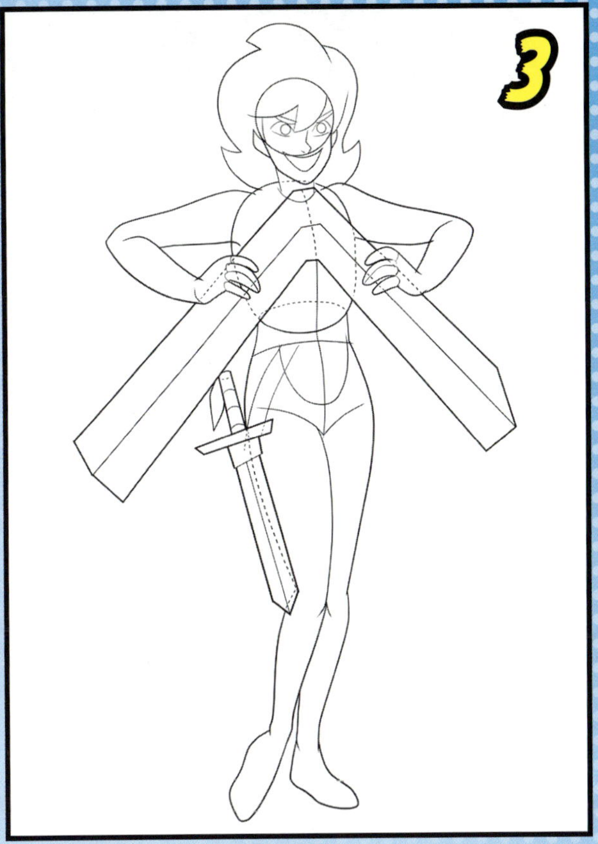
3
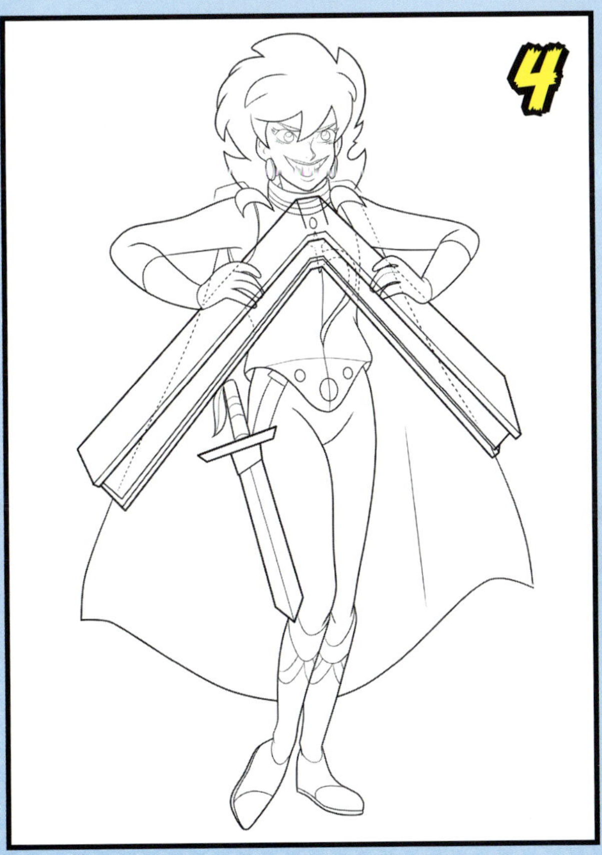
4
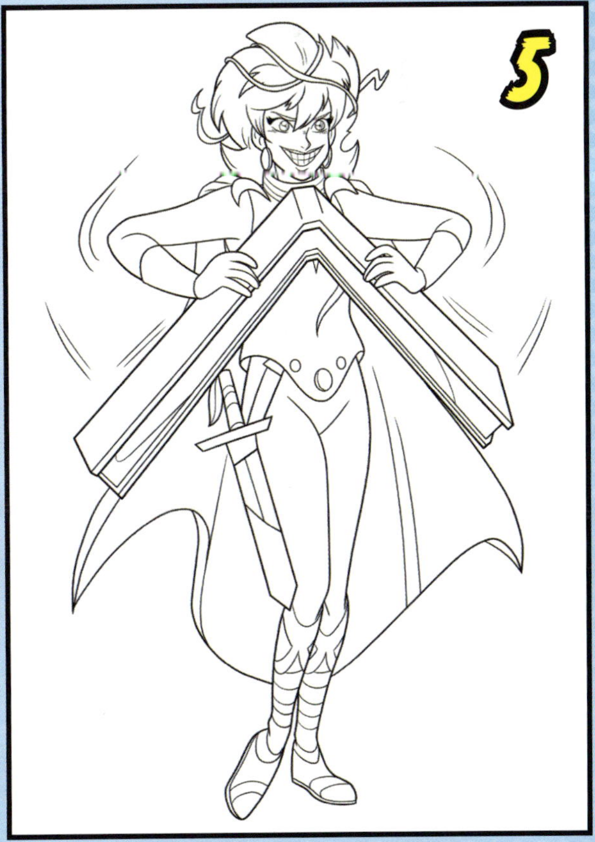
5

MORGAINE LE FEY

Stay out of the way of Morgaine le Fey! The evil sorceress from King Arthur's time is a masked menace. Telepathy, spell casting, and youth absorption—yeah, she can drain your youth to restore her own—are just a few of her talents. And if she's backed into a corner, beware! Morgaine's mystical energy bolts can blast you into the past!

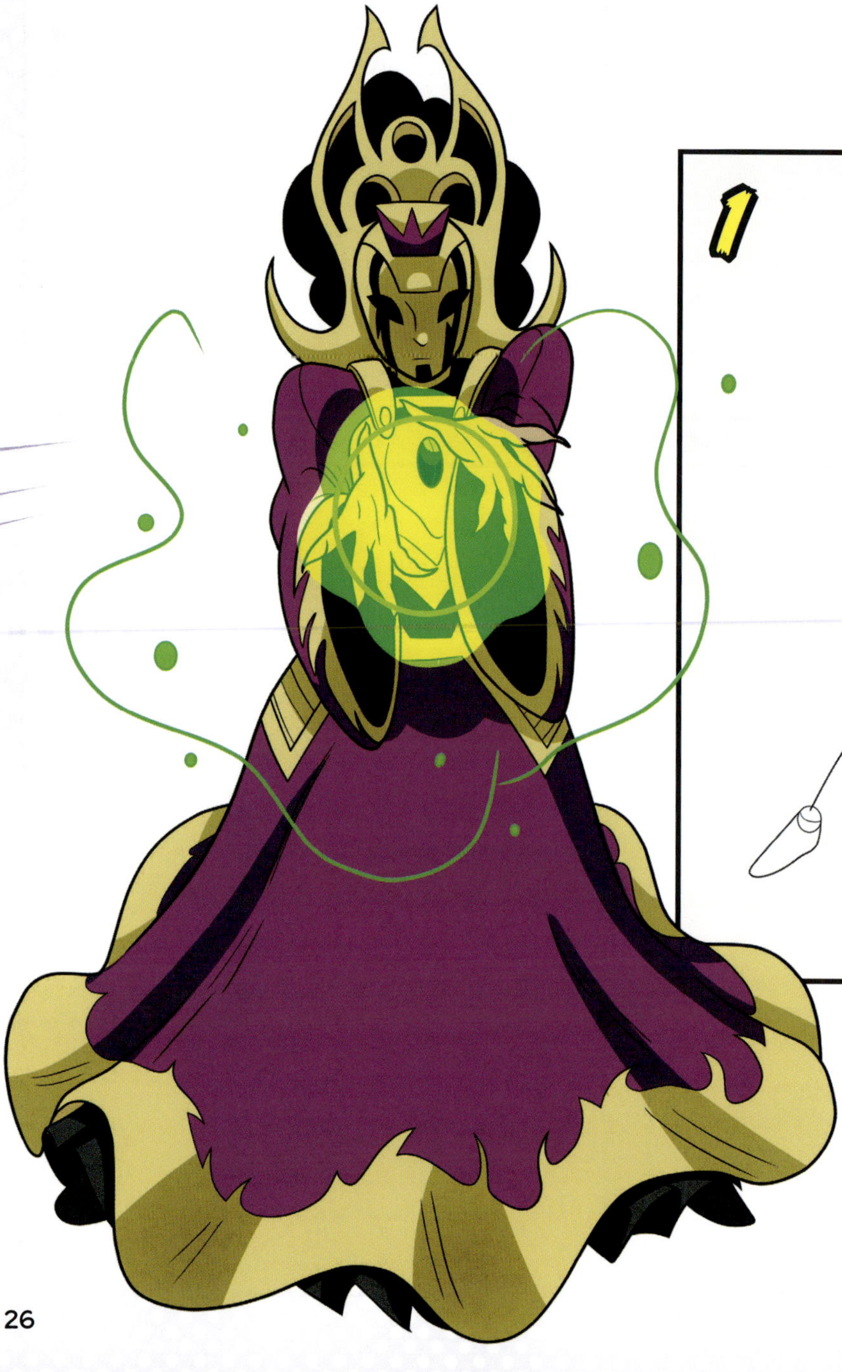

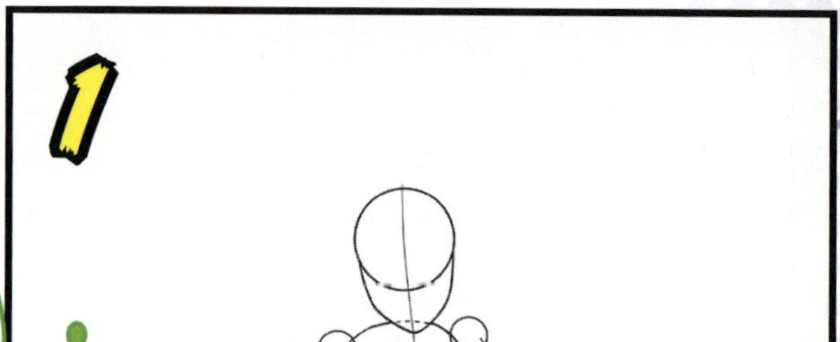
1

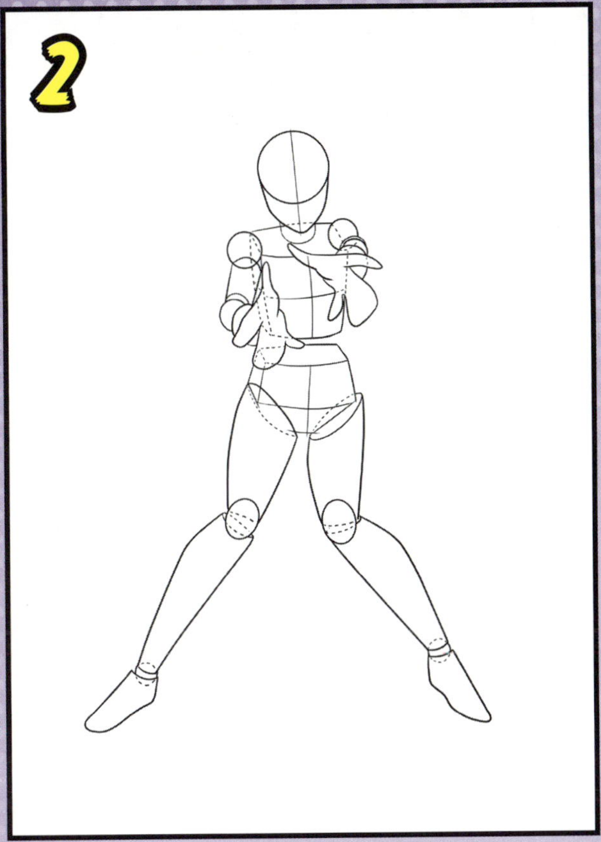
2
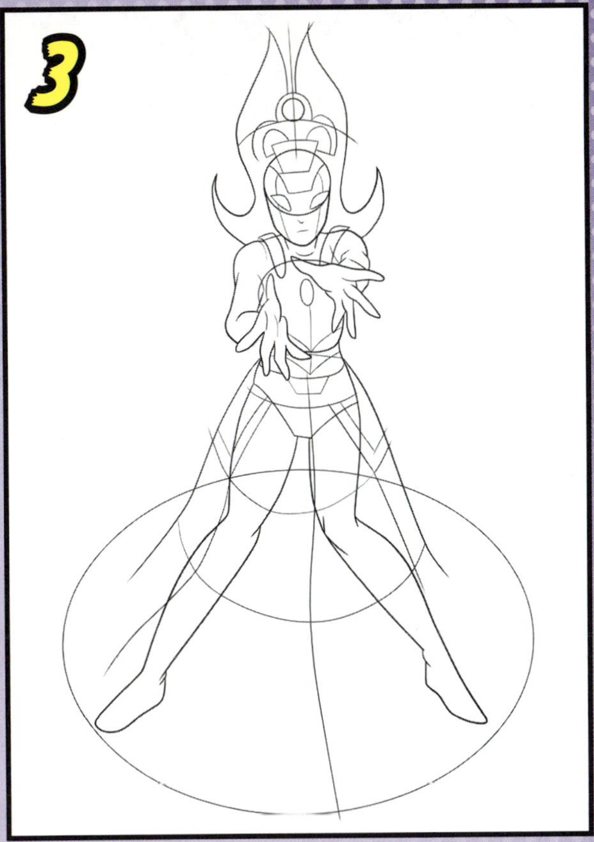
3
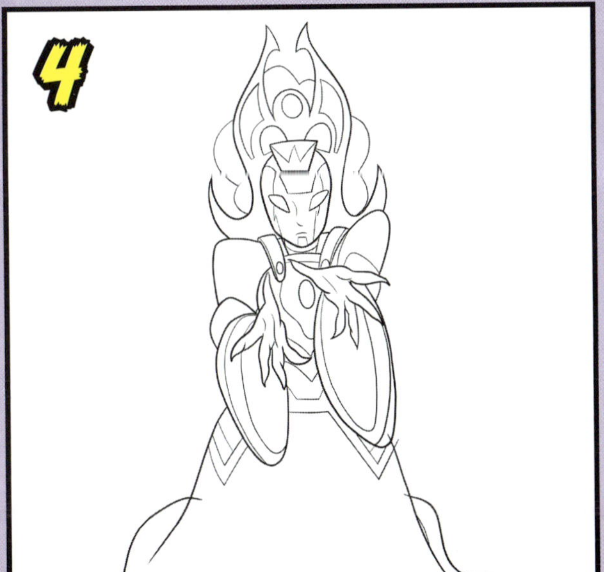
4
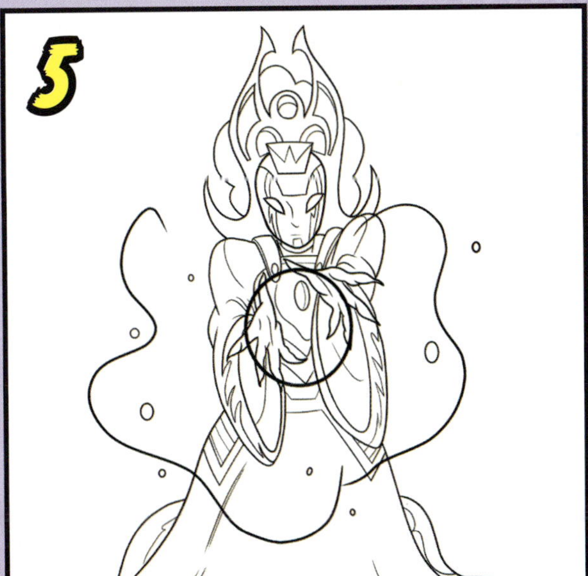
5

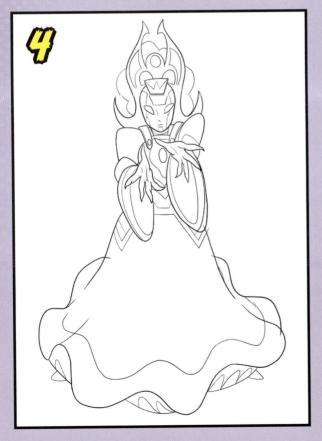

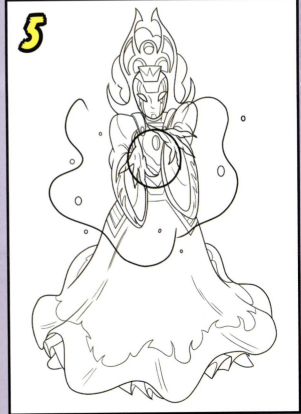

WONDER WOMAN VS. GORILLA GRODD

Uh-oh! Gorilla Grodd is up to no good in Gateway City! Can Wonder Woman survive the super-smart ape's attack? Or will her Amazonian shield buckle under the brutal bashing? YOU ARE THE MANGAKA. THE FATE OF THE AMAZING AMAZON IS IN YOUR HANDS!

MANGA FACT
Rumiko Takahashi is a legendary female mangaka who has created several best-selling series. Among her most well-known are *Ranma ½*, *Inuyasha*, and *Maison Ikkoku*.

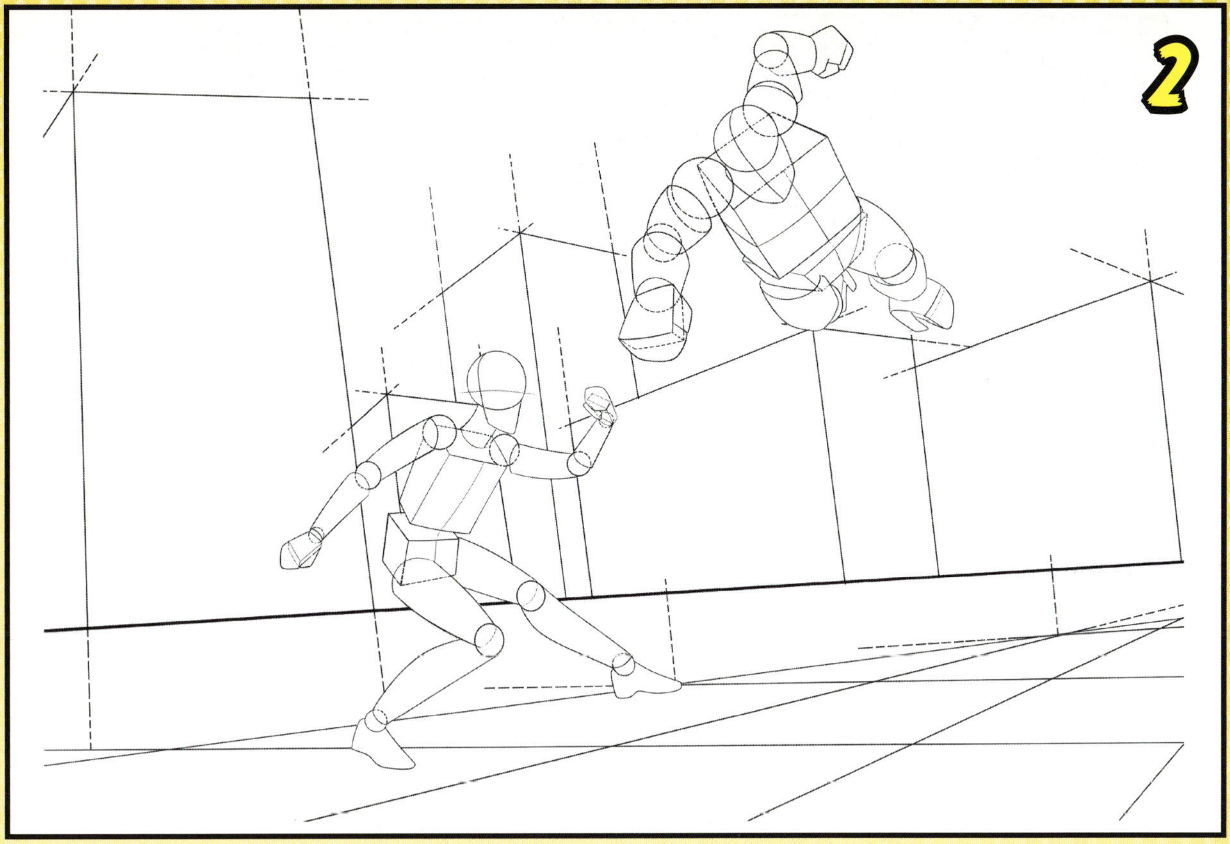
2

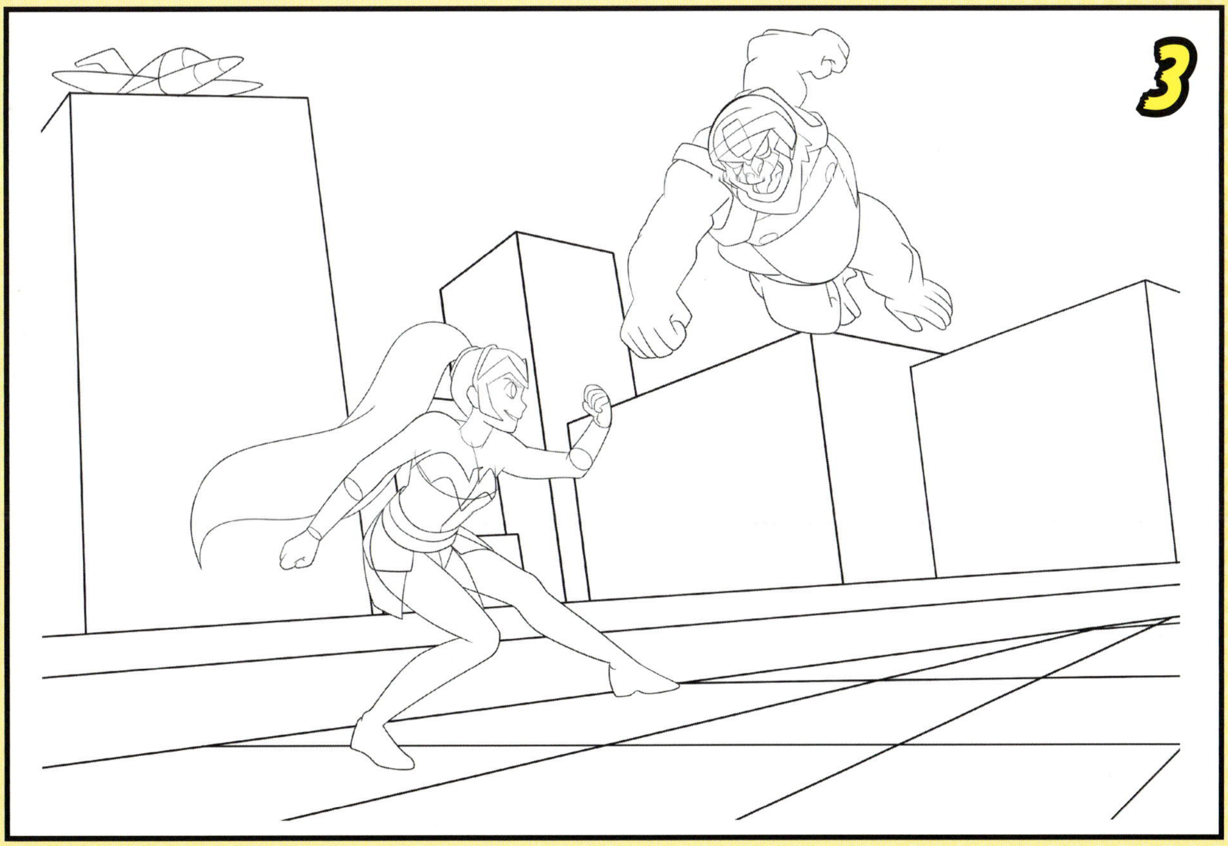
3

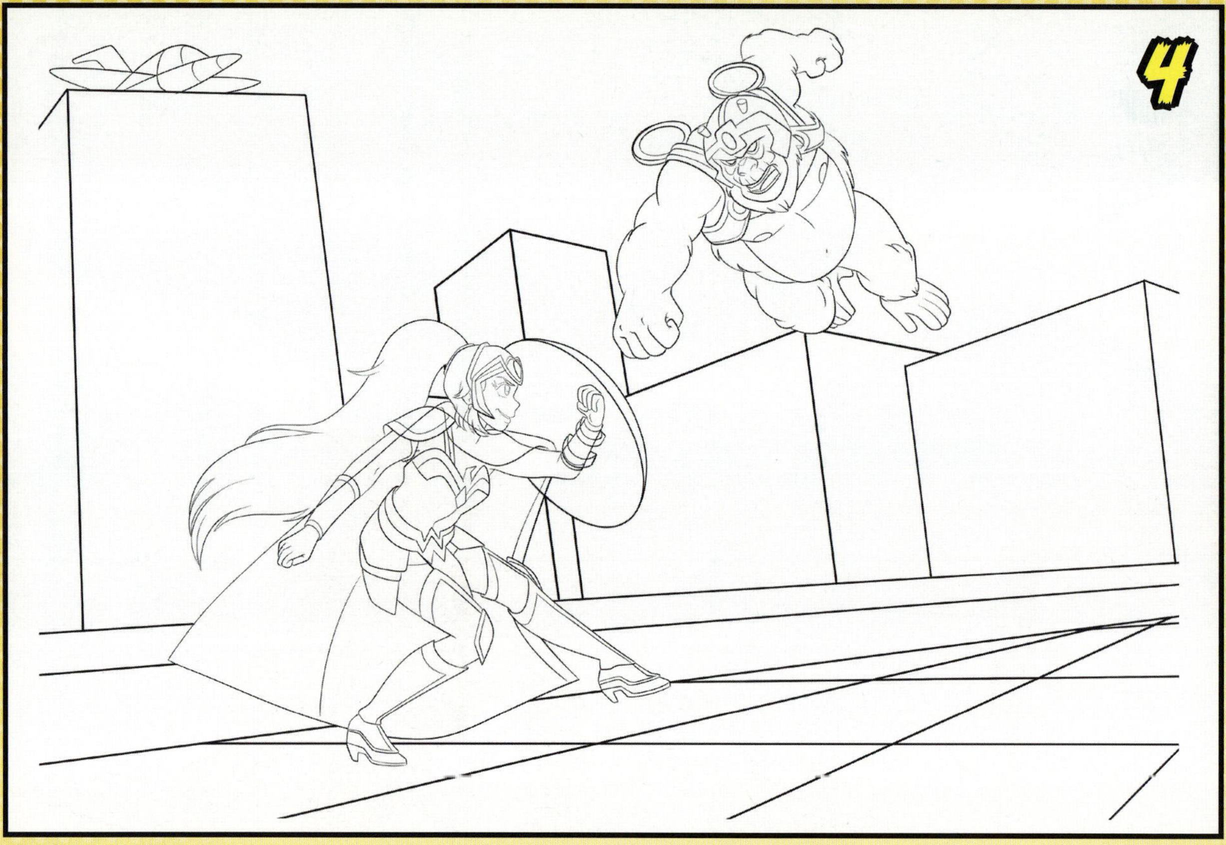
4

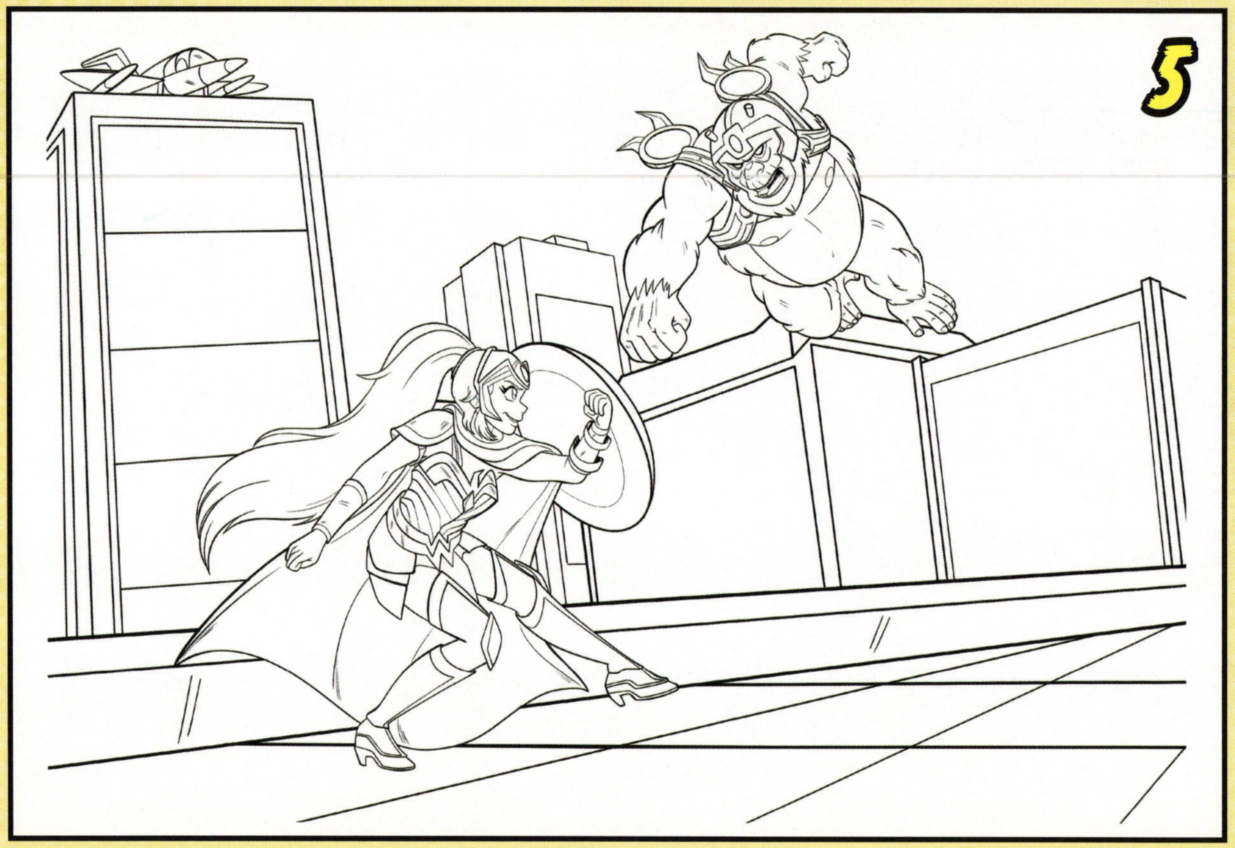
5

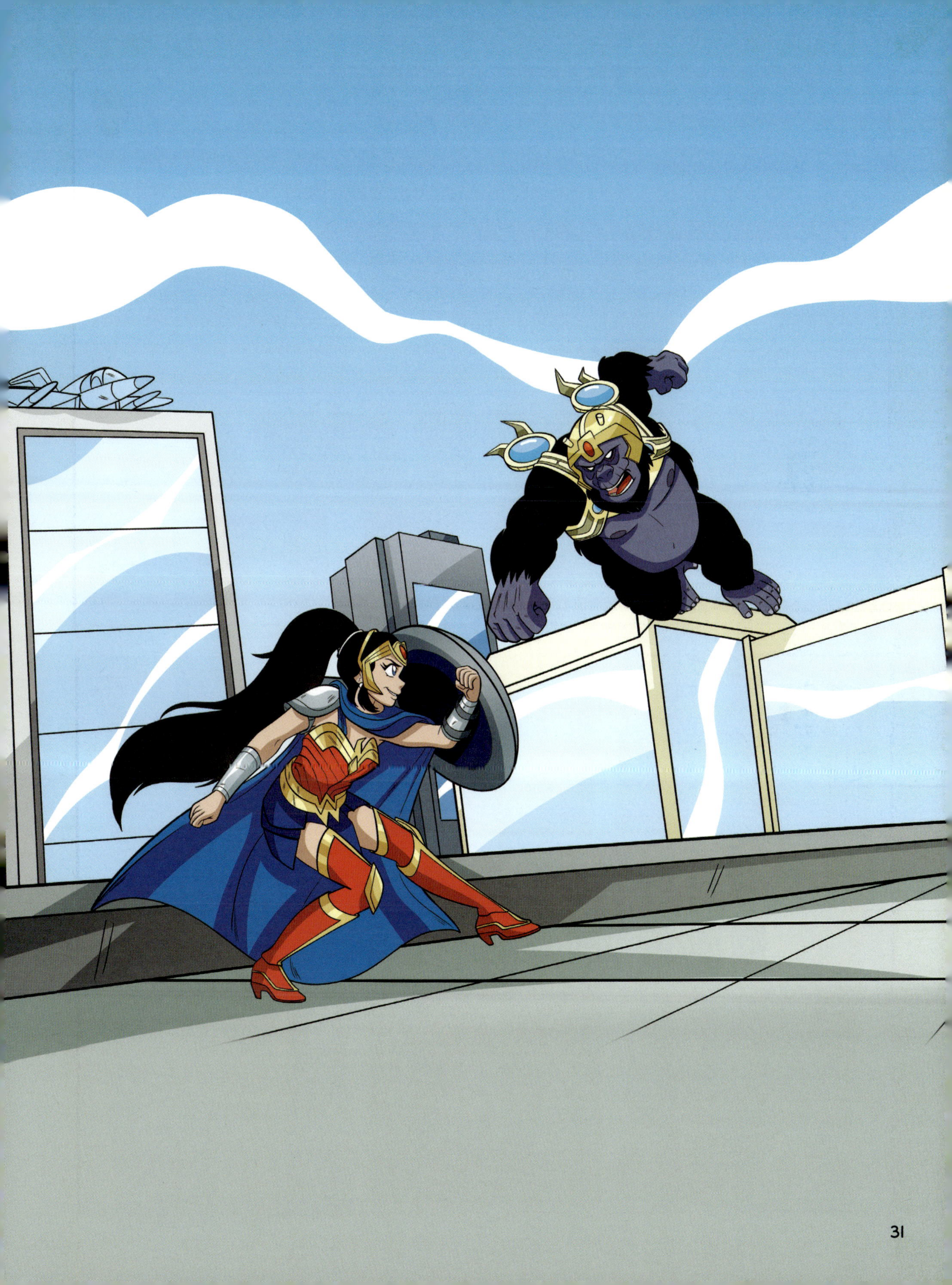

MORE MANGA DRAWING FUN!

Hart, Christopher. *Drawing Anime from Simple Shapes: Character Design Basics for All Ages.* New York: Drawing with Christopher Hart, 2020.

Whitten, Samantha. *Let's Draw Manga Chibi Characters.* Beverly, MA: Walter Foster Jr., 2023.

Yazawa, Nao. *Drawing and Painting Anime & Manga Faces: Step-by-Step Techniques for Creating Authentic Characters and Expressions.* Beverly, MA: Quarry Books, 2021.

MORE DC SUPER HERO FUN!

Wonder Woman
ORIGAMI
AMAZING FOLDING PROJECTS FEATURING THE WARRIOR PRINCESS
BY JOHN MONTROLL

DC SUPER HEROES
SCHOOL JOKES
BY MICHAEL DAHL & DONALD LEMKE

WONDER WOMAN
AN ORIGIN STORY

YOU CHOOSE
WONDER WOMAN
THE CRYSTAL QUEST
12 POSSIBLE ENDINGS

DC SUPER HERO
FAIRY TALES
THE AMAZON PRINCESS AND THE PEA
Sutton · Garbowska · Brys

WONDER WOMAN
THE AMAZING AMAZON
CHEETAH UNLEASHED
SNIDER · VECCHIO

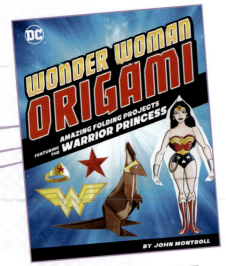

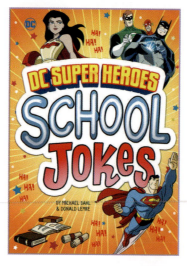

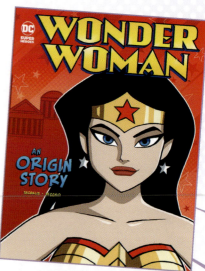

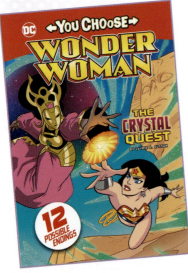

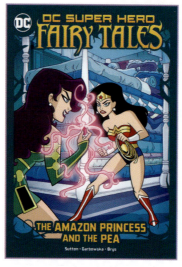

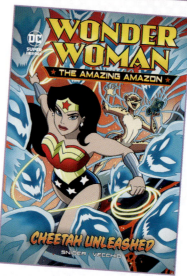